Planning & Remodeling

Bathrooms

**By the Editors of Sunset Books
and Sunset Magazine**

Lane Publishing Co.
Menlo Park, California

We gratefully acknowledge...

the homeowners, architects, and designers who have shared with us their experiences in bathroom design and construction, and who have allowed us to share their own most personal rooms with you. Special appreciation goes to architect Thomas A. Abels for his valuable consulting assistance.

Cover and above: *Sparkling tile bath—built into a storage room of a 60-year-old house—made a suite out of the master bedroom. Joined to the bedroom by a common wall, the new bath makes excellent use of a sharply sloping ceiling: see how on one side of the room the tub lies along the lowest wall (2½ feet high), and then how generous the headroom is in the 10-foot-high shower (see cover). To achieve a custom look, standard basins were given porcelain enamel painted fittings, and tiles were laid in the floor in crisp, sophisticated diagonals. Architect: William B. Remick. Photographed by Jack McDowell.*

Book Editors:
   Barbara Gordon Gibson
   Maureen Williams Zimmerman

Staff Researchers: Kathryn Arthurs,
                   Donice G. Evans
Design: Roger Flanagan, Kathy Avanzino Barone
Illustrations: Terrence Meagher

Editor, Sunset Books: David E. Clark

Contents

Special Features

Revitalizing the bath

- **Decorate, remodel, or build?**
- **Getting help** • **Money matters**
- **Plumbing**

There's at least one almost universal fact of contemporary Western life: almost everybody has a bathroom. And, primitive though some may be, it's a matter of common assumption that at least one bathroom comes with every house that's bought, sold, or newly built. "Sorry, we don't have one" just isn't a response we generally hear when we ask our host or hostess directions to the bathroom.

Taken for granted as they are, however, bathrooms—and bathing in particular—haven't always been so customary. True, 5,000-year-old plumbing systems have been discovered in Crete, and Romans used to bathe together by the thousands. But it wasn't really until the Victorian era that bathrooms came to be separate rooms in the house. Abstinence from bathing was widespread in the Middle Ages, and during the reign of Queen Elizabeth I (who bathed only once a month), few baths were found in houses. Even the White House waited until 1850 to get its own bathtub.

Updating the basic bath

Today, most of us view bathing and bathrooms as enjoyable necessities. Testifying to the increased interest in improving and personalizing the bath are small shops and large sections in department stores specializing in bathroom accessories, as well as plumbing suppliers who offer countless variations in the color, shape, and size of bathroom fixtures.

The ideas presented on the following pages were selected to help you personalize your own bath, whether you choose to remodel or simply redecorate. When you consider them, keep your mind open to new ideas; they may not be as costly to actualize as they appear. And as you look closely at the bathrooms that appeal to you the most, consider what it is you're responding to: Is it the color scheme? Fixtures? Interesting tile pattern or use of wood? Some of the things you like best may fall handily into your own bath plan.

Also consider the type of bathroom you could most enjoy. Do you want it small and enclosed or open and spacious? Will it be shared or private? A single room or compartmentalized? Would you choose a bright, sunny bath, or one that's cozy and softly lighted? Would you like lots of things to see and touch around you, or do you prefer a tidy, uncluttered bathroom?

Utilitarian needs must be met, too. Your bathroom might be the only one in a house inhabited by several people. Or it could be one of several in a large house. The number of people who will be using a bathroom—their ages, habits, and needs—is information vital to planning.

In your present bathroom, what are the features you dislike and want changed? What do you want to accomplish by redecorating, remodeling, or adding a new bathroom? How will that bathroom relate to the rest of the house? What future needs can you foresee?

Thinking through these questions and any others you can come up with will be an invaluable aid when you begin to decide on the elements in your new bathroom.

Will changes be extensive?

It's helpful to think of a bath redecoration or renovation or the construction of a new bath as an opportunity to achieve new comfort, beauty, and convenience. Simply adding new accessories or a fresh coat of paint can do much for the appearance of an old bathroom at a relatively small cost. New tiling or carpeting will rejuvenate an outdated bathroom; new shelves and cabinets can relieve irksome overcrowding.

For any type of change, begin by gathering as much information as you can on design ideas and the newest materials, fixtures, and accessories. Then work up a budget based on the parts of the job you think you can handle, the going local rate for skilled help, and the estimated cost of materials.

The answer may be decorating . . .

Though it's part of remodeling, decorating doesn't include structural changes. Its cost can range from modest to extravagant. Simple accessory changes can often revitalize a tired bathroom—a new color on the walls for an impression of spaciousness or brightness, or a new throw rug, shower curtain, and coordinated towels to add pattern. Certainly decorating is the quickest and most convenient way to visually change a bathroom.

Decorating is as individual as people. As in revamping any other part of the house, "rules" are made to be broken. However, some general guidelines that have proved successful for others may be helpful to you.

First, choose a background color for the walls, ceiling, and floor. Work around the existing fixture colors—match or complement them. The background color need not be the same tone on all surfaces. Changeable color accents in the room can be provided by matching or complementary towels, rugs, and other appointments. Consider color, pattern, and scale of all the bathroom components before making final decisions.

One aspect of bathroom decorating that's often overlooked is the relation of the bathroom colors to other rooms nearby. It's usually pleasing to decorate a small powder room in the same colors you're using in the adjacent foyer or entry hall or to coordinate a master bathroom color scheme with that of the master bedroom and possibly the dressing room.

. . . or is remodeling the approach to take?

Remodeling usually involves more than surface changes. Your goal might be a limited modernization or a dramatic rearrangement of space. The project could range from replacing tile and fixtures to enlarging an existing bathroom or converting a different type of room into a bathroom. Sometimes the addition (or subtraction) of a partition or wall will markedly transform a bathroom's overall appearance.

Homeowners may be surprised to find that remodeling can often cost more than adding on an entirely new bathroom. What contributes to the cost is the extra labor involved for demolition before beginning new building,

the restrictions of working within set measurements and structural elements, and—especially in older houses—the difficulty of knowing exactly what wires or other structural complications you're going to discover and then have to work around.

Many of the exciting features going into new bathrooms can be included in a remodeled one. But before you take a skylight idea from one source and a vanity design from another, make sure their designs work for the room as a whole—and that they work well with the design of the rest of the house.

In most cases the best way to begin remodeling is to draw a to-scale floor plan of your present bathroom, including the exact sizes and shapes of the fixtures. If the remodeled bathroom will include or affect other rooms, those rooms and their features should be on the floor plan, too. It's also helpful to make scale drawings of the walls. If you know the location of existing water supply and waste lines, you should include them, too.

Before you begin removing walls, plan the total project as completely as you can, down to details of locating ventilating ducts, heating ducts, light fixtures, storage cabinets, and mirrors. And calculate how much time it will take to complete your project, how to dispose of the materials and fixtures you tear out, and how to move such awkwardly shaped components as shower stalls and bathtubs in and out of your house.

To avoid the most common remodeling headaches, do these things: 1) Estimate time, money, and other factors as exactly as possible; 2) Know as much as you can about your community's plumbing and building codes, regulations, and guides (contact the city or county building department, mechanical and electrical inspectors); and 3) Have written agreements with whomever you employ to do work for you, including prices, general descriptions of fixtures and materials, and a statement that places on the installer the liability for an unsatisfactory installation or fixture damage.

Look for before-and-after examples of remodeled bathrooms on pages 8, 34-39.

If it's a new house

When you're planning a new house yourself or consulting an architect or designer, you have considerable choice in the location, type, and style of bathrooms. Of course, a bathroom's design shouldn't clash with the architectural style of the house.

Try to consider personal needs and desires you may have that might require more than the stereotyped, 5 by 8-foot, three-piece, standard bathroom package could provide. The standard package may be your ultimate choice, but don't settle for it without first looking into other possibilities.

Bathroom location theories vary. Where you locate your bathroom will be determined by available floor space, the needs of family members, and the number of bathrooms in the house. A common practice is to place fixtures back-to-back when two bathrooms are on the same floor, and above and below each other when they're on different floors. This way, plumbing can be shared by many fixtures. Doing this generally results in saving some money—but not always a large amount.

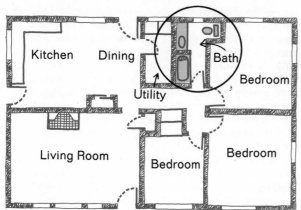
Typical placement of single bathroom in one-story house.

There are sound conceptual and economic reasons both for clustering sinks, baths, and toilets and for the alternative of separating them. Clustering is usually less expensive, but it might not be convenient or functional for you.

If the house will have only one bathroom, a logical choice is to position it between the public parts of the house (living room, entry) and the sleeping and dressing areas so that it is convenient to both sections. In a house that will have two or more bathrooms, placing one of them adjacent to a sleeping and dressing area is a popular choice.

In a 1½ or 2-story house, the bathroom is usually located on the second floor. For safety, avoid placing an upstairs bathroom next to or at the head of the stairs.

Building codes must be considered in planning bathroom location. For example, codes usually state that a bathroom can't open directly to a kitchen; the two rooms must be separated by a hallway or by two doors.

In a development house, your options on design, plumbing fixtures, and other details depend upon the particular builder, his method of doing business, and, in some instances, how much you're paying for your house.

Some builders start with a basic plan and specifications and offer several options throughout the house, much as an automobile dealer will give you options of color, engine size, and so forth. Other builders—even those in the higher price categories—have developed standard plans for which they've organized purchasing and construction methods so they can build with maximum efficiency and economy. Because of the way they're organized, these builders can offer few, if any, options.

Getting the help you need

If you're redecorating you might consult an interior decorator; if you're remodeling you'll probably work with a carpenter and plumber; if you're building a new bathroom, you may employ a plumber, a contractor, and an architect.

Each of these specialists can help you by offering knowledge and skills that would take you years to acquire for yourself. Try to be aware of precisely what they can be expected to do for you, as well as what their limitations may be in relation to your specific project.

How much can you do yourself?

This is a question only you can answer. On the positive side, you can achieve great satisfaction by acquiring and using the skills you need, saving quite a bit of money, working at your own pace and at times that are convenient for you, and knowing the job was done with care and is up to your standards of excellence.

The negative aspects of doing the work yourself include the time you'd spend away from other activities that you enjoy more, the demands of having to solve vexing problems, the effort of learning the skills and estimating and buying the exact materials and tools you'll need, the possibly extensive physical labor of doing the work, and the potential need to hire someone to finish the job for you anyway.

Almost every remodeling project has a few easy, do-it-yourself opportunities. If you've done some projects before and enjoyed them, you can work on parts of the job yourself and leave other parts to specialists. But if your plans include plumbing, heating, air conditioning, or electrical work, be sure to check local ordinances before starting the work yourself. Permits will probably be required, and code compliance will be demanded. The regulations may require that certain portions of the job be done by licensed workmen.

For help in do-it-yourself projects, see manufacturers' instructions; these often are well illustrated and very complete. Many products on the home improvement market are specifically designed for installation by the homeowner. Since manufacturers and dealers want satisfied customers, they will probably be glad to answer specific questions. Your local government building department is another source of detailed and specific information. Articles and ads in home-oriented building and remodeling magazines can be helpful, and the Sunset books *Basic Carpentry Illustrated* and *Basic Plumbing Illustrated* are particularly good references.

Architects. . . and related professionals

An architect is a highly trained specialist in combining organization, esthetics, and practicality in construction. He designs and draws up plans for buildings and supervises construction.

If you're contemplating any kind of structural change, an architect can give you an individualized, custom design and save you time and money in the long run. He can help you with such things as how to get the most service out of the floor space, how to introduce natural light, how much storage to allot, and how to cope with bearing walls or other obstacles that might stand in the way of enlarging a bathroom.

You can employ an architect for all or part of a number of services. Here's what the architect will do: 1) Discuss and organize your basic needs and make rough sketches of practical solutions; 2) Draw up precisely detailed plans and specifications for bids, obtain the building permit for a new house (the contractor usually handles permits in remodeling), and ensure that nothing contradicts local codes and ordinances; 3) Supervise the contractor's work as it progresses, seeing that the requisite grades of materials and workmanship go into the job and that time schedules are met; and 4) Make a final inspection of the completed work and sign a certificate of approval when you and he are completely satisfied. Unless retained on a consultation basis specifying an hourly fee (the usual procedure in remodeling), architects generally work on a flat percentage basis tied in with the total cost of the job.

The best way to choose an architect is to inspect his work. Many licensed architects belong to a professional organization, the American Institute of Architects (AIA), which has a referral service. Look in the Yellow Pages under "Architects" for the address and telephone number of the nearest AIA chapter.

A building designer can be someone who has an architect's education and training but hasn't gone through the state's licensing procedure. Or he may be a member of a relatively new profession of building designers that has a separate educational program and a professional organization called the American Institute of Building Designers. The AIBD can refer you to a building designer on the basis of your location and the type of job you're contemplating. Check your telephone book for the address of an AIBD office in your area.

A building designer will provide you with preliminary drawings for a minor fee and a set of plans for a prearranged price. The designer will make constructive suggestions concerning your plan and help smooth out any rough edges.

A draftsman can be either an unlicensed, apprentice architect or a member of a skilled trade prepared to draw plans exactly according to your instructions. If you are experienced in building and know such things as which electrical conduits to specify, exact requirements for joists and studding, and the pros and cons of various fixtures, you could save money by hiring a competent draftsman at an hourly rate. To locate a draftsman, check the Yellow Pages under "Building Designers" or "Draftsmen."

A general or prime contractor

If your project will involve a number of subcontractors—such as plumbers, carpenters, electricians, tile setters—it might be to your advantage to use a reliable licensed general contractor. Contractors who do a large volume of work can buy materials for you at low wholesale prices. However, if the job is small, you may have difficulty finding a contractor willing to take it on because larger projects are more profitable for him.

In much of the bathroom remodeling being done, though, almost all of the work is handled by a single contractor/carpenter—a jack-of-all-trades who can carry out some plumbing tasks as well as carpentry.

Although doing your own contracting will certainly save you money, it will also eat up a lot of your time. You'll have to get in touch with, choose, and supervise the skilled workmen and cope with the fact that they often have strict union rules, such as a set working sequence.

To find a contractor or other skilled workers, talk with homeowners who have had work done. You can also check with subcontractors and material suppliers or a bank or local credit bureau.

When selecting a contractor, keep in mind that the one with the lowest bid is not necessarily the one who will do the job best. You should base your choice on his reputation in home building—he should be cooperative, competent, and financially solvent. He is the one who orders the materials and hires, supervises, and coordinates the work of the various subcontractors.

You should get in touch with at least two (and preferably three) contractors for a preliminary cost estimate on a major project. Though there is no fee or obligation of any kind on your part and no firm commitment on theirs, you'll have a basis for further planning.

After all major and minor decisions have been made, the contractor can give you a firm bid. Then a complete, legal, written contract should be prepared. The contract should include dimensions, specifications, and type and quality of all materials, as well as a time schedule, cleanup agreement, bankruptcy release, and payment agreement. Usually a contractor is paid either on the installment plan, voucher system, or in one lump sum upon completion. After you've made a thorough inspection, you acknowledge completion of the job in writing.

To build tub, *owner nailed exterior paneling over contoured extensions of wall studs and insulation, finished wood with fiberglass cloth and three sanded layers of resin.*

Subcontractors: plumbers, tile setters, electricians

Whether or not to hire skilled workmen for all or part of the work is a decision that should be made early to avoid scheduling problems. If you plan to hire out most of the work, be sure you have the time and determination to act as your own general contractor; if not, hire a licensed one. The services of a plumbing contractor or other subcontractor include supplying current product information, selling fixtures and supplies, advising you, and doing work in accordance with technical drawings and specifications that comply with local codes.

At first glance the services of skilled workmen may seem expensive. Yet they have the specialized tools, training, and experience to finish the job much faster than you could, and you can expect a professionally finished job from them. Using skilled workmen can even save you money if you weigh it against the cost of your own time.

If you're acting as your own general contractor, you must know how to get the most from the people you hire. Often they're accustomed to the routine of doing a job in one particular way and do not welcome changes. For example, if you want the niche for the soap dish inset high in the shower wall to keep spray from the shower head from reaching it, you'll probably encounter resistance from the tile setter who wants to position the niche where he's used to putting it.

Trade associations can recommend licensed subcontractors on the basis of your location and the type and extent of work involved. Check the Yellow Pages under "Plumbing Contractors," "Electric Contractors," and "Tile-Ceramic, Contractors" for the address and telephone number of the local branch of the trade association. Recommendations from other homeowners will also help you to locate subcontractors.

When dealing with subcontractors, make sure you supply clear instructions, have all firm agreements in writing, know what's realistic to expect, and provide as much direct supervision as you can.

An interior decorator or designer

These specialists in the decorating and furnishing of interiors offer professional skill in making the most of what you have. Beyond that, they supply fresh, innovative ideas and interpretations and provide access to unique materials and products.

Usually, homeowners contact a particular interior designer on the basis of personal recommendations or because they've seen and liked work by the designer in magazines, books, or at a show house. Membership in a professional organization called the American Society of Interior Designers (ASID) is one assurance that a designer is well qualifed. Check the Yellow Pages under "Interior Decorators & Designers" for the telephone number and address of the ASID chapter in your area.

Interior designers work on a very individual basis; their approaches often differ, too, according to the type and size of a specific job. A preliminary interview is customary to see whether the homeowner and the designer can work together effectively, communicating about each other's taste and ideas. Interior designers usually either charge a professional fee (hourly rate) or take a percentage of the cost of the merchandise used.

Before (below): Shower stall on left was removed, as was built-in chest on outside wall. After (right): Space under the house and low drainage lines allowed the tub to be recessed and placed against new window wall.

How much bathroom can your money buy?

The amount of money you spend determines, to a certain extent, the bathroom you'll end up with. The most obvious effect of economics on the bathroom is its standard 5 by 8-foot size. Then, too, a certain amount of standardization has been necessary in the bathroom fixture industry to keep costs down. But creating an outstanding, out-of-the-ordinary bathroom doesn't have to be a severe strain on your budget.

How to calculate expenses

Early in your planning, you should determine the amount of money you can reasonably afford to spend in building a new bathroom or redesigning an existing one, based on discussions with a building designer, architect, or contractor. Keep in mind your plans for the future. Along with present expense, consider future mortgage and later remodeling possibilities. With a new bathroom, your house will be more valuable. A new bathroom may be the first stage of a long-term remodeling project.

It's wise to prepare a complete budget and list of materials before you buy anything. The time you spend researching costs and calculating specific prices will save you time and money later.

On the list of materials, include an implementation schedule and the exact cost of the materials you need. Select alternatives to your first choices—you may find a particular item has been discontinued or is available only after a months-long wait. Time is perhaps the most difficult cost factor to estimate for each phase of work and for the whole project; this is particularly true if you're planning to do part of the work yourself.

To determine costs accurately, refer to a scaled floor plan and wall elevations to calculate the exact quantities of materials you'll need. A mail order catalogue and a few telephone calls can give you quick price estimates. Describe your entire project; if the total cost of materials is substantial, the supplier will probably offer a discount. In most instances the cost of labor will be from 60 to 75 percent of the total cost of materials, but a reputable local contractor can give you a more precise estimate based on your materials list.

The sales tax on building materials shouldn't be overlooked in planning costs—it may be substantial. It's deductible from your income tax when you're acting as your own contractor.

Financing your new bathroom

An important consideration in most extensive bathroom remodeling and building projects is how to finance the work. The ideal way is to anticipate the project a few years in advance, open a special savings account, and deposit a given amount monthly. This allows you to begin your project when your target date arrives, saving you a substantial amount of interest.

Loans of various types for home improvements are available from several sources. Because terms and interest rates vary from one locality to another and

sometimes from bank to bank in the same community, it's worthwhile to shop around.

Commercial banks, savings banks, and savings and loan companies are usually the best places to consult. Consider especially FHA home improvement loans available through these sources and other special loan programs sponsored by local or federal government agencies. A loan arranged through a contractor is usually more costly than a loan taken out directly by the property owner.

Other possibilities include borrowing against a life insurance policy or from a company credit union and mortgaging or remortgaging a house.

Once you have a rough idea of how complicated the construction job will be, you can confer with a loan officer. Although at this stage the lending institution won't be able to commit itself on exact amount, terms, or interest, the loan officer can give you the bank's "rule of thumb" regulations governing modernization loans. Since each institution has its own rules governing the amount and length of loan and rate of interest, investigate thoroughly before making your final decision. When you have a completed set of plans and a specific bid on the work, you can settle exact arrangements.

Plumbing—underneath it all

Behind (and underneath) every successful bathroom is some plumbing. An understanding of the mechanics of a plumbing system will help you better plan a new bathroom or a remodeling project. (For more detailed answers to plumbing questions and for information on do-it-yourself plumbing, consult the *Sunset* book *Basic Plumbing Illustrated*.)

Know your plumbing system

"Plumbing" includes all the piping and piping accessories needed to bring water into and through the house and then take water out of the house. Each plumbing fixture is connected to a supply of water. Each of these fixtures is also connected to a drain system that carries the used water away.

The basic in-out circuit becomes more complex when a fixture requires both hot and cold water and when several fixtures are connected to the same supply and drain pipes. In addition, if the drainage system is to function correctly, it must be vented to the atmosphere through special vent pipes. These vent lines increase the apparent complexity of the overall system.

Supply. A house's water supply system consists of pipes and fittings in carefully planned sizes, assembled on the job site or prefabricated in a shop.

A supply main carries water under pressure into the house from the public water main outside. Then the supply main delivers the water to one or more supply branches or risers, which in turn divide at the water heater into hot and cold-water subsystems. Pipes for the two usually run parallel throughout the house. The supply main contains a house shutoff valve and a water

Money-saving plumbing hints

As you plan, be aware of plumbing economies. In the total budget of a house—and to an even greater extent in a remodeling project—plumbing is an expensive item. Generally, fixtures, fittings, and labor will cost more than lines of pipe.

Here are some ways to economize as you're planning the plumbing:

• Place new fixtures close to existing pipes to minimize extra carpentry and plumbing.

• Locate kitchen plumbing on one side of a common wall and bathroom plumbing on the other.

• Do as much work as possible at one time, while the pipes in the walls are exposed.

• Have existing plumbing checked for weakness, catching trouble before it starts.

• If you anticipate future changes, rough in the pipes to avoid opening walls a second time.

• If possible, plan upstairs and downstairs plumbing on the same wall, again to save extra pipes and carpentry.

• Use qualified plumbers who guarantee the results. If you're doing the job yourself, remember that plumbing

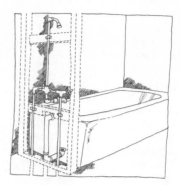

must pass the local building department's inspection. Otherwise, you may have to rip it out and do it over again.

See an architect, designer, builder, or plumbing contractor for additional money-saving possibilities. If you want to save by doing your own plumbing, see the *Sunset* book *Basic Plumbing Illustrated* for detailed directions.

---

meter. The branches and risers have individual room shutoff valves marked "hot" or "cold."

• *Hot-water systems.* These are of two basic types. In one, the water is heated instantaneously in a boiler and continuously circulated in a loop pipe system by a pump to give immediate hot water at the outlet. In the other type, water is heated and then stored in a tank for future use. The need for hot water is usually estimated to be one-third of the need for cold water.

• *Pipe materials.* Galvanized steel is the traditional material for water pipes. Copper tubing, though usually more expensive per foot, is also widely used since it is normally easier to install. Plastic pipe is easiest for a do-it-yourselfer to work with. In addition, it doesn't corrode, it insulates well, and it may be less expensive than other kinds of pipe. The disadvantages of plastic pipe are its noisiness and a tendency to sag. Then, too, some local building codes don't allow plastic pipe, or they allow it only for drain-waste-vent lines.

• *Exposed pipes.* Although plumbing is usually concealed, it doesn't have to be. Left exposed, it can suggest the kinetic processes that make the house work; it can also be the basis for decorative experiment. In Europe, exposed hot-water pipes are often used as towel racks/warmers. The main drawback to exposed

plumbing is added expense—it must have a more finished appearance than concealed plumbing.

Drain-waste-vent. Used water leaves each fixture through a drainpipe, which is part of the system that handles water drainage, waste removal, and venting.

At each fixture the drain passage contains a U or S-shaped bend called a "trap." This trap retains water that acts as a seal to prevent gases and bacteria from entering the house.

Each fixture is also vented—connected to vertical pipes (stacks) that carry off sewer gases, bring in fresh air, reduce corrosion, and keep the whole drain-waste-vent system at the atmospheric pressure necessary to maintain the water seal in each trap. Vent stacks extend through the roof, where they open to the air.

The toilet vent pipe, called the "soil stack," often serves also as the main vertical waste line. The term "wet venting" is applied to this system for venting and draining waste water through the same vertical pipe. Revents or back vents connect secondary vents from other fixtures to the soil stack above the level of the highest fixture in the house. The soil stack connects with the main house drain in the basement or crawl space.

The main house drain is a large horizontal pipe that transports used water and wastes from the soil stack and other drainpipes to the house sewer outside. Since the waste and drainpipes work by gravity, they must be planned and fitted with special care. Strict code requirements govern pipe size, vent/fixture offset, and other factors.

When you're replacing fixtures

As a preliminary step, it's a good idea to consult a plumbing contractor to determine whether or not the existing piping will work satisfactorily with the new fixtures you're considering. Sometimes the age and condition of existing piping require that it, too, be replaced along with the bathroom fixtures.

Even if the pipes are in good shape, you're likely to run into some snags if you live in a house that's more than 15 or 20 years old. If new fixtures have slightly different dimensions, you'll have to make some changes in the house's internal plumbing as well as at the outlet.

See the information about each specific type of fixture (pages 24-28) for additional hints.

Installing and extending plumbing

Installing plumbing for a house addition or converting a room to an extra bathroom involves installation of water-supply and drain-waste-vent piping in walls, floors, and ceilings. This preliminary work is called "roughing in."

If you're going to extend existing plumbing, try to work around the existing waste lines and soil stacks. Relocating them can be very costly and, in some instances, virtually impossible. In a home built on a concrete slab, for example, the waste lines and base of the soil stacks are embedded in the concrete and would have to be cut out to relocate the fixtures. In homes with crawl space or sufficient area under the bathroom floor, these lines can be relocated, but it's an expensive process.

The maximum wet-vented distance between the fixture trap outlet and the soil stack is specified by the National Plumbing Code according to pipe diameter; however, each community has its own rules and regulations. Always plan piping layouts to take the most direct route, avoiding obstacles wherever possible.

Factory-made plumbing core. In some areas you may be able to purchase a factory-made plumbing core that will provide ready hookups for bathroom, kitchen, and laundry fixtures. These prefabricated sections are sometimes open-stud walls that are quickly nailed in place as a plumbing wall of a house. In other instances these cores are complete rooms that are lowered onto subflooring to provide both a finished bathroom and plumbing hookups for kitchen fixtures. Local builders and building supply firms can tell you whether these units are available in your area and whether they conform to the local building code.

Water pressure. It's advisable to check available water pressure when planning an additional bathroom. One way to do this is to turn on several faucets in the house for a few minutes. If the pressure drops noticeably, the outside water supply may be inadequate and larger pipes may be needed. Or deposits in the old supply pipes may reduce available pressure, necessitating replumbing the house supply system.

Hot-water supply. Another factor to consider in remodeling a bathroom or adding another is the size of your water heater and its recovery rate. An average 2½-bathroom house with an automatic washer and dishwasher requires at least a 50-gallon hot-water tank. Each manufacturer of hot-water supply tanks has his own method of calculating the storage capacity of tanks for families of different sizes and different hot-water demands. They all publish tables that can be used to judge the size of the tank required.

Future needs. Anticipating future remodeling when you're building a new house can save you money later. For example, if you intend to eventually finish a basement as a family room with half-bath or to add an attic bedroom and bathroom sometime in the future, you can run plumbing to the area, cap it, and wait to install fixtures later. Roughing in plumbing during initial construction is cheaper than adding supply and drain-waste-vent installations in a finished house.

Plumbing codes differ

Every community's building codes are different. A book of suggested guidelines—the *Uniform Plumbing Code*—might help answer some of your plumbing questions. *The Uniform Building Code* is another good reference; your local laws may be stricter, though.

Most areas require ventilation for an interior bath and, in some areas, a marble slab as the toilet base, marble baseboard trim, and ceramic floor tile laid over metal lath and mortar. In some cases the latter requirements are waived on the basis of an "existing condition." But you may find yourself having to put down a ceramic tile floor first before you can lay carpeting.

It's wise to have your own copy of the local written regulations and to ask the building inspector specific questions before beginning your project.

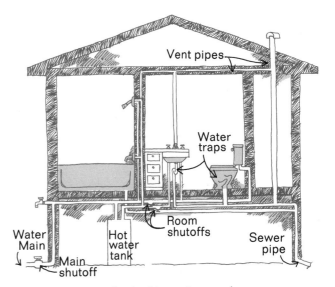

Basic components of a plumbing system are shown.

The comfort factors

- **Natural lighting**
- **Electric lighting, wiring, outlets**
- **Heating** • **Ventilation**
- **Soundproofing**

A comfortable, functional bathroom depends on good lighting, ventilation, heating, and sound control. Maintaining a desirable physical atmosphere in a bathroom calls for certain special approaches.

Windows and skylights

These panels of glass or plastic connect a walled-in bathroom with what's outside, and this connection—which functions in both directions—affects the bathroom's light level, movement of air, temperature, visual effect, and auditory effect. Without windows, mechanical bathroom ventilation is a necessity.

Opening windows can cool off a hot, steamy bathroom. Windows can bring in a garden view and garden sounds. In addition, the natural light from windows and skylights, coupled with bathroom humidity, will encourage plants to thrive in your bathroom, adding to its attractiveness. Reflections and views from windows and strategically placed skylights can make a bathroom seem much larger than its actual size.

About glass and plastic

You'll find many kinds of glass and plastic to choose from for bathroom windows and skylights. Each type has its special purposes, its own advantages and disadvantages. If you use tinted, patterned or stained glass, pay particular attention to its effect on your total decorating and color scheme. Degree of light transmission and heat gain and loss are the most important features to consider. In specific locations where safety is a factor, local building codes will probably define the kind of glass to be used.

Clear glass. Standard clear and transparent window glass brings the maximum amount of daylight—as much as 88 to 90 percent of what's outside—into the bathroom. It's the most common and least expensive type of glass.

Insulating glass. Insulating glass consists of two sheets of glass with a dry gas or dry air space sealed between them. The outer sheet of glass may be tinted.

Usually, an insulating glass unit with $1/2$-inch air space will reduce heat loss through the glass area by about one-half. Just as insulating glass will block some heat loss from the bathroom on cold days, so will it also reduce heat input on hot days. To further reduce heat transmission, order the glass with a reflective surface.

Insulating glass will reduce condensation, also. By keeping indoor glass surfaces warmer on cold days, it permits indoor humidity levels to go quite high without causing condensation. New types of insulating glass with a special reflective coating insulate like three sheets of glass, permitting still higher indoor humidity before condensation occurs.

Reflective glass. From the outside, reflective glass has a mirrorlike appearance. But from the inside you can see through it. Such glass cuts down the amount of heat transmission by as much as 70 percent while reducing light transmission by 50 to 70 percent. It also reduces glare and ultraviolet transmission.

At night, *glass panes coated with reflective, metalized polyester film become usable overhead mirrors.*

During daylight hours *you can see out through a comfortably "tinted" window (below), but people outside can't see in (right). The metallic film reduces heat, glare, and fading caused by the sun's ultraviolet rays. Architect: Pat Coplans.*

You can have an aluminum-coated polyester film applied over the inside of already-installed clear glass areas to increase reflection and thus reduce solar transmission. The manufacturers claim it rejects 75 percent of the sun's heat and about 80 percent of the glare.

Tinted glass. This type of glass blocks much solar radiation—though part of it is soon reradiated to the inside as heat. Tinted glass also provides more privacy than clear glass, with little impairment of the view to the outside.

How much does tinted glass alter colors? When you're looking outdoors from within, gray-tinted glass provides very natural color retention. Bronze may make the outdoors appear slightly brighter while actually reducing light intensity, but most people observing the outdoors through it will be unaware of any change in color. Green-tinted glass slightly intensifies green colors and tends to make the outdoors look cooler.

It's possible to apply a tinted coating to glass in existing windows. Several companies manufacture spray-on or flow-on tinting products that reduce both glare and solar heat and repel fabric-fading ultraviolet rays.

Patterned glass. You can use this type of glass in a bathroom where good light is required yet privacy is important. The degree of privacy is determined by the pattern you choose; many patterns and textures are available. Patterned glass is also desirable because of its light-diffusing properties. If safety is a factor, use tempered or wired patterned glass. Patterned glass is also available in colors and with a glare-reducing finish. Plastic panels come in patterns, too.

Stained glass. This glass is used primarily for its interplay of color and light; stained glass also ensures privacy. Color, style, and subject matter of stained glass panels vary widely. Blown glass is more expensive and has richer color with more variations of shade and thickness than machine-pressed glass.

Sound control glass. Made with thick plastic layers laminated between two sheets of glass, sound control glass reduces sound transmission.

Safety glass and plastic. Most communities require that safety glass or plastic be used in all areas that could be hazardous, such as framed and unframed sliding glass doors, fixed glass panels less than 18 inches above the adjacent floor (they could be mistaken for doors), and shower doors and tub enclosures. Materials specified include fully tempered glass, wired glass, laminated glass, and rigid plastic. These won't break readily—and if they do, the chances of bad cuts are minimal.

• *Tempered glass.* This glass is three to five times stronger than untempered glass of the same kind and thickness, and not much more expensive. You can get tempered glass in sheet or plate, clear or patterned, plain or tinted types. Measurements for custom tempered glass must be exact; the material can't be recut once it goes through the tempering process.

• *Wired glass.* Wire mesh incorporated in the glass holds it together if broken. It's widely used (and widely required) in skylights. There are several different wire patterns.

Generous fixed panes *of glass, plants create feeling of showering outdoors. Architect: Carl Day.*

Corner window *of mitered glass overlooks private yard. Architect: Raymond L. Lloyd.*

Shoji screen *made from plastic panels hinged to old window frame allows light and privacy.*

• *Laminated glass.* Clear or tinted vinyl is sealed between two pieces of clear or patterned glass. If the glass is broken, the plastic inner layer holds the glass together. Cost is high and not competitive with that of tempered sheet glass for residential installations.

• *Plastic.* Rigid clear, patterned, or tinted panels with a high shatter resistance are often used in windows, room dividers, doors, and skylights. Sizes and thicknesses vary. Plastic panels aren't as cleanable or abrasion resistant as glass, but they're less likely to shatter and easier to work with and install.

How to use windows

To give maximum benefit, windows should be thoughtfully placed, and they should be the right size and style for the particular bathroom. For example, it often isn't practical to put a large window over a bathtub, for the window will be difficult to reach to open and close and can cause drafts. If windows are used over a tub, they should be installed high enough to allow privacy and also be above the shower spray level.

A bathroom window should be easy to open and close for ventilation and temperature control, and it should be screened to keep out insects.

Windows on southern and eastern sides of a house bring in more light and solar heat; the north and west sides will receive less intense sunlight. West sun can be the most difficult to handle; east sun is the most desirable because it warms the bathroom in the morning.

You could try windows on two bathroom walls for cross ventilation. But try to avoid having bright light streaming through a window directly onto a mirror.

Window styles. Windows for a bathroom can slide horizontally (generally the most economical), slide vertically (double-hung), swing from the side (casement), swing from the top (awning), or pivot vertically (projected).

Some architects have made a point of separating fixed glass—for seeing through—from the opening for air, which then comes through separate louvers. If you plan a garden next to the bathroom, you could open an entire wall to the view with a combination of fixed glass and a sliding glass door and screen.

Generally, maintenance of bathroom windows is easier if they have aluminum rather than wood frames, particularly in climates where sticking and swelling can be a problem.

Window decoration. Window treatments of many sorts can be used in the bathroom. Among the possibilities are shutters or louvers, Roman shades, woven blinds, or curtains. The only real limitation is that ruffly, delicate materials tend to suffer from humidity. Tightly woven fabrics like duck, sailcloth, and denim are sturdier.

Various devices can be used to call attention to a glass area that might be a safety hazard. Decals come in many designs; paste-on muntin strips running horizontally across a door or window, two to four feet above the floor, are easy to see, especially if they are 2 or more inches wide and metallic or brightly colored.

Plants, chairs, or open storage units are effective in front of glass walls and windows. Mobiles, hanging panels of stained or colored glass, or wire sculptures are decorative in front of glass panels and call attention to them as well.

Should you add a skylight?

Skylights are an exciting way to bring in natural light and open up the bathroom visually, especially if you have a windowless interior bathroom or privacy problems. Skylights combined with windows can create exciting effects.

You can avoid the three possible problems with skylights—leaks, heat loss, and difficult maintenance—if you choose the skylight carefully.

Types. Check your local building codes regarding approved kinds of glass and plastic, how much area the skylight can cover, and other possible restrictions. Skylights are available in clear and colored plastic and in glass domes as well as in glass block units set in frames. Most residential skylights are manufactured in units complete with frames. Commercial greenhouse sections make great skylights, offering variety of design and the option of opening and closing. Successful installation, though, may be more difficult.

Translucent plastic domes are the most common form of factory-made residential skylights. They cut down the strong light that a clear skylight would admit to a room, and the domed shape tends to be cleaned by rainfall. On the other hand, clear skylights are effective if you want to look up at the clouds or at tall trees, and they admit about 85 to 92 percent of available light.

Flat glass or plastic skylights are sometimes used on sloping roofs, but they increase the amount of glare and heat in the bathroom unless they admit only north light. A flat skylight requires more cleaning than a domed one.

Condensation on the inside of a skylight can be a problem in winter or in cold climates; double-glazed dome skylights prevent condensation and also reduce heat loss. Most skylights have gutters to drain off condensation. In a windowless bathroom, use of a ventilating fan will lessen the skylight condensation problem.

Installation. Proper installation of a skylight is essential—otherwise it's almost sure to leak. Some units can be purchased ready for installation, requiring only that you cut a hole in the roof, set the skylight in place and anchor it, and then install the roofing material over the skylight roof flange.

If a skylight is oriented east or north on a sloping roof, it won't let in much hot afternoon sun. In cases where a skylight must face south or west, a shade or blind can be used to reduce heat and light intensity.

Electric lighting, wiring, outlets

Bathroom lighting should be both practical and decorative. Good lighting can create a feeling of spaciousness; an otherwise cramped, drab bathroom can be made to seem larger and more inviting through a change in the lighting arrangement.

Plans for lighting the bathroom should begin in the blueprint stage of a remodeling project because lighting is difficult and expensive to add later. To keep costs

Sunshine *from small skylight floods through warm golds and ambers of stained-glass panel. Designer: Robert Wendt.*

down, don't change light fixture locations—behind-the-walls rewiring is costly. When new light fixtures are added, it's advisable to have an electrician verify that the new unit won't overload the existing circuit.

Bathroom lighting falls into two basic categories: general illumination of the room as a whole and lighting for specfic areas. The two should be balanced to avoid glare. A light level of 30 footcandles is recommended by engineers for bathroom lighting. In nontechnical terms, this is the equivalent of 3.5 to 4 watts of incandescent lighting per square foot of floor area or 1.5 to 2 watts of fluorescent lighting.

Overall illumination

Diffused, ambient, overall lighting helps prevent glare. The source of general lighting can be a complete luminous ceiling, a luminous panel, track lighting, or a single, effective ceiling fixture. Ceiling fixtures are often quite decorative and can be combined with a vent fan or with an infrared heat lamp.

The safest way to handle overhead lighting is to wire it to a switch just outside the bathroom door.

Relation to room decor. The colors and textures used within the bathroom have an important effect on the lighting. Dark colors absorb light; white fixtures and light walls reflect and diffuse light, reducing shadows.

If there's a lot of contrast between light and dark in your bathroom, you should try to compensate by raising the amount of general light. Do this with additional fixtures rather than with brighter bulbs. Be especially careful that wattage isn't too strong if you're using shiny, glossy, and metallic-look wallpapers.

Use wall, ceiling, and floor surfaces in your lighting plan—they reflect and diffuse light, helping to control the actual amount of light. Matte surfaces reflect a pleasing, diffused light that is generally glareless. Some wood interiors, such as paneling and cabinets, can be bleached or given a light wash of paint to improve their reflective qualities without hiding the grain. If you have a lot of light-swallowing dark surfaces, you'll have to add enough light to overcome the lack of reflection.

Luminous ceiling. When the entire ceiling is the light source, there are few if any shadows and the bathroom seems more spacious. The luminous panels and grid supports are ideal for lowering a too-high ceiling or hiding ceiling imperfections.

A luminous ceiling usually consists of fluorescent tubes or incandescent bulbs attached to the ceiling, a grid of aluminum or wood strips 6 to 12 inches below the tubes or bulbs, and plastic or glass panels set into the grid. Luminous ceilings can usually be hung with nothing more sophisticated than hand tools. This type of lighting can be purchased as a packaged unit or it may be custom designed. Some packages come complete with heaters and ventilating fans for installation as one unit.

Single luminous panel. A circular or rectangular luminous panel can be attached to a regular electrical outlet in a ceiling for streamlined wide-source lighting.

Track lighting. Versatile track lights can be adjusted to reflect off walls for diffused illumination or to spotlight a particular area where you need more light.

Single ceiling fixture. Single-source lighting arrangements can work well in a small bathroom. A chandelier or other distinctive fixture can be used decoratively.

Localized lighting

Different fixtures have been developed for the different areas in the bathroom that have special lighting requirements. Mirrors—which are usually located over the sink—have the most specific requirements. Tub and shower enclosures also require special lighting.

If the bathroom is compartmentalized, each compartment should be well lighted, which means an additional light over the toilet. Special bath adjuncts—such as gym equipment, saunas, and steam rooms—may require special illumination.

Don't make localized lighting too bright. If you can't look directly at the fixture, or if you see an afterimage when you look away, the lights are too bright. Use diffusing methods such as frosted bulbs or frosted glass or plastic panels, or bounce the light off a wall. Better yet, install additional sources of lesser-intensity light.

At the mirror. Light for grooming should be soft and diffuse, without glare or shadows. Mirror lighting should be directed toward the person in front of the mirror rather than toward the mirror itself. Lights that shine directly on the mirror tend to blur the image and give dazzling reflections. Lights along both sides of the mirror, in addition to a ceiling downlight, will usually give an accurate mirror image. The lighting from the sides is important—overhead lighting alone can cause deceptive shadows.

Lighting above the mirror might be a row of bulbs (theatrical lighting), a long fluorescent tube or incandescent bulbs behind a diffusing panel or on a soffit, or a single decorative fixture. Extra lighting above the mirror is really necessary only if the general overhead light is less than adequate or if the side lights are far apart.

Diffusing panel *softens light from fluorescent tubes or incandescent bulbs, can be used for side-lighting, too.*

When one or two basins are installed in a vanity counter more than four feet wide, try several 75-watt incandescent bulbs or two rows of fluorescent tubes running the length of the mirror and counter, installed on a soffit that's at least 15 inches from front to back.

The lights on the sides of the mirror can be vertically mounted tubes behind diffusing plastic or glass, a row of bulbs, or other fixture style that suits the bathroom's decor. In most cases, side lights can be added without changing the wiring. Widely available surface-mounted fixtures can be wired into the existing fixture. Swag lights use a decorative chain to disguise obvious cords.

Theatrical lighting—*rows of bulbs first used in actors' dressing rooms—supplies an accurate, shadowless reflection.*

The decorative effect you want and the degree of efficiency you need will influence your choice of light fixtures. Ordinarily, all three light fixtures—the one above and the two beside the mirror—are controlled from one wall switch.

Tub and shower lighting. An auxiliary light is a good idea for most tubs and showers, especially if you have opaque doors or a heavy shower curtain. Special moisture and steam-resistant light fixtures, circular or rectangular, can be recessed into the ceiling over the shower or tub. These lights must be UL approved for use in tub and shower areas. Be sure to place the light switch so it's out of reach of someone using the tub or shower.

Toilet light. If your bathroom is compartmentalized, you'll need an additional light for the toilet enclosure. In either an open or a compartmentalized bathroom, a reading light is also convenient. A wall source or ceiling downlight with a 50-watt incandescent bulb usually works well. Rewiring might be necessary if you add a toilet light.

Incandescent or fluorescent lighting?

This choice depends on the general effect you want to create in your bathroom, the need for bright light in certain parts of the room, and your personal preferences. Incandescent bulbs provide the most flattering light; fluorescent tubes produce more light at less wattage, conserving energy.

Incandescent bulbs are more like sunlight in effect. White bulbs are usually best for bathrooms because tinted bulbs or shades can distort colors.

Fluorescent tubes extend light in a line. Check with a dealer to find out which kinds are best for use in a bathroom. Fluorescent bulbs come in different shades, some more flattering to skin tones than others.

As a pleasant compromise, a combination of incandescents and fluorescents can create a soft but adequate glow throughout the room.

Special types of lights and lamps

Some lights are combined with a fan, heating element, or both; others can be connected with a sun lamp. Check for special wiring codes that must be followed for heat lamps or sun lamps.

Heat lamps are ideal for instant warmth when you step out of a shower or tub. They'll heat a bathroom during the cooler portions of seasons when the regular house heating is turned off. Follow the manufacturer's recommendations when installing and operating heat lamps.

Ozone lamps aid in freshening the air. These lamps should be mounted above eye level, as they should not be viewed directly.

Sun lamps can help you keep a year-round tan. Follow the manufacturer's recommendations for installation and use of the lamps. You might investigate ceiling fixtures that include fans, ultraviolet heat, and sun lamps. Several manufacturers make combination fixtures that permit sunbathing while one shaves or dresses, with timers as auxiliary devices to guard against overexposure. These fixtures can be recessed into the ceiling.

Night lights are helpful in any bathroom to prevent stumbling in the dark, and are especially practical in children's bathrooms. Dimmers are available to provide varying levels of light. With fluorescent lighting, special dimming ballasts are required.

Electric outlets

While you're planning your wiring, be sure to consider outlets for all the electric appliances you might want to

Platform behind bathtub *folds down (above) to allow sunbathing under ultraviolet and heat lamps. Large acrylic skylight provides a view.* **Unobtrusive** *platform (right) folds up, disappears in wall. Architect: Brett Hanville.*

Small fireplace *warms bathroom for bathers, removes steam condensation from mirrors. Architect: Fred Hummel.*

use in your bathroom. These may include electric shavers, electric toothbrushes, hair dryers, curlers, and facial saunas. Think about storage for these appliances at the same time you're planning the electric outlets. Will they be out on the counter or in a vanity or medicine cabinet near the outlet?

Heavy-duty outlets for heaters and other equipment that draw considerable current should also be planned in advance.

All electric installations must be in accordance with local electric codes, and electric appliances should be used with caution. Codes usually require a minimum of one grounded electric outlet (near the basin) per bathroom.

Safety considerations

Switches for lights should be located so that they can't be operated by anyone using the tub, shower, or lavatory. Placing a switch for an overhead light just outside the entrance to the bathroom is a good idea. The electrical cords for any appliances used in the bathroom should be in top condition, and a grounded connection should be provided for use with electric appliances.

Any changes made to the lighting system must conform to the local electric code requirements. Every bathroom has the potentially dangerous combination of water and electricity, so follow every precaution.

Heating your bathroom

What could be worse for early risers than a cold and drafty bathroom? Be sure the heating arrangements will be adequate. Pay special attention to the areas where

heat loss will be greatest: along exterior walls and in front of exterior doors and windows.

For extra luxury, some people like to step out of a tub or shower into the warmth provided by a nearby heat lamp or sun lamp (see page 17). Another touch of comfort comes from putting a towel rack next to a heat register so towels will dry quickly and be warmed.

Extending central heating

If you build an addition to house a new bathroom, you may be able to run the furnace ducts to this new room and make it a part of your central heating system. But it's advisable to check your present furnace's heating capacity and duct sizes to determine whether or not the existing heating system can handle the additional load. You might have to consider separate heating.

Supplemental heaters

If wall heaters or other supplemental heating units are used, place them so that people aren't likely to get near enough to burn themselves and so there's no possibility of towels or curtains catching fire. In general, portable heaters shouldn't be used, for safety reasons.

Any electric heaters should be safely wired with appropriate grounding to prevent electrical shock. A thermostatic control is recommended so the heater will shut off at a given temperature. If you use a gas heater, make certain it's properly vented and has a safety pilot shut-off.

A fan-assisted ceiling heater is usually adequate for blowing heat around small areas for short-term warmth.

Heated ceiling

A radiant ceiling heating system consists of gypsum wallboard with an insulated resistance wire imbedded in the core. It warms *objects* rather than the air; secondary heating occurs as air moves across the warmed objects and is heated by convection. You install this clean, noiseless system using ordinary drywall construction methods; electrical connections and thermostat installations are done by an electrician. A radiant ceiling can be painted, papered, or textured.

Providing good ventilation

Proper ventilation will help prevent such minor inconveniences as fogged mirrors and such major problems as moisture penetrating the walls. To control odor, toilet fixtures are available with built-in venting arrangements. Ozone lamps are also effective in eliminating odors in the bathroom.

Natural ventilation

Doors and windows have until recently been the main sources of bathroom ventilation. Using them consumes no energy, but the overall room temperature changes when they're opened.

Bathroom ventilation fans

Ceiling or wall fan

Ceiling fan with infrared heater

Ceiling fan/light combination

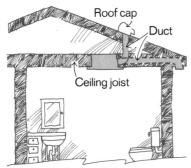

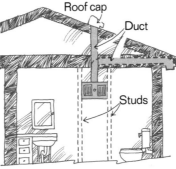

Ceiling fan *is installed between ceiling joists, ventilates through ducts either to roof, eave, or outside wall.*

Wall fan, *installed between the studs on an inside wall, also ventilates through ducts to roof, eave, or outside wall.*

Wall fan *ventilates directly outside when installed between studs on an outside wall.*

Good cross-ventilation will result from well-thought-out placement of screened windows in combination with transoms or other vents which open and close. Partial partitions will increase air circulation.

Fans

A ventilation fan is needed (and often required by building codes) in most bathrooms—particularly in bathrooms without windows. Fans are especially necessary in humid climates. The fan should discharge directly to the outside, either through specially built ducts or a passage that's part of a purchased fan unit. Minimum-capacity rating suggested by ventilation engineers is 12 complete air changes per hour.

Many ceiling or wall-mounted ventilation units are on the market. Most bathroom fans are one-speed, though fans with up to five speeds are available. Some fans are quieter than others; "squirrel cage" fans are generally much quieter than bladed fans. Fans come fitted with heat lamps and/or regular lamps for general room illumination.

An exhaust fan can operate on its own switch (perhaps with a timer) independently from bathroom light fixtures, or it can operate on the same switch as the light. Check local building codes regarding which electrical wiring and ventilating arrangements are approved. Some codes specify that, in a windowless bathroom, a ventilator must go on automatically when the light switch is activated.

Ways to soundproof

Walls built to provide sound control between the bathroom and adjoining rooms are a feature to consider when you're building or remodeling a bathroom; they can muffle the sounds of running water and reduce pipe noises.

The best way to control sound is to plan for it before the walls are constructed. A framing design that uses slit studs, staggered studs, or double wall studs will reduce noise. A partition system with accordion-folded gypsum wallboard between the walls also gives efficient sound control. And blanket insulation applied between the studs will lessen bathroom noise transmission through a solid wall into an adjoining room. Pipes shouldn't touch the studs or the wall surface.

The wall surfacing material (usually gypsum wallboard or plaster) should be thick. For even better soundproofing, add gypsum backer board or sound-deadening fiberboard.

Other aids to sound control include a plumbing system that has been properly sized, with pipes not isolated from the fixtures and with drainpipes slanted to slow the flow of water. In addition, you can wrap noisy pipes with several thicknesses of asphalt building paper and overwrap them with fiberglass insulation.

Other noise control measures include using a solid door and thicker glass (or even special sound control glass) and installing airtight resilient weatherstripping around doors and windows that open to the outside. Avoid undercutting a door for ventilation—such cutting aggravates any noise problem.

Unfortunately, most bathroom materials that are both easy to clean and waterproof are also hard surfaced so they reflect and echo noises. But there are exceptions: ceilings, for instance, can be constructed of materials that are both sound-absorbing and moisture resistant, and washable carpeting is a quiet flooring. Finally, you could create a pleasing auditory situation by piping sound from a radio or stereo into a bathroom with a ceiling-mounted speaker.

Fixtures & materials

- **Floor plans** • **Basins**
- **Toilets, bidets**
- **Tubs, showers**
- **Floor, wall, ceiling, counter finishes**

The first step in designing a new or remodeled bathroom is to plan the placement, style, and color of the plumbing fixtures (basin, bathtub, shower, toilet, and bidet). They take priority because they're the most permanent design elements and may well be in use for the lifetime of the house. Then decide on a floor of tile or carpet; counter of marble, tile, plastic laminate, or wood; and papered, painted, or tiled walls that complement the fixtures.

Fixtures and materials for use in the bathroom are available in great variety. Most manufacturers offer five or more fixture colors. Select the colors of fixtures and materials with care, keeping in mind that the type of lighting you use—fluorescent, incandescent, natural—will alter the colors. Remember: specific colors change from manufacturer to manufacturer; even whites vary.

Take time to search out fixtures and materials with the special features you would most like to have in your bathroom. New design developments in bathroom fixtures and materials are occurring constantly. Dozens of special-use fixtures and materials are offered to help meet individual space and layout requirements.

Fixture placement: floor plans

The "best" bathroom floor plan doesn't exist—good plans vary according to the bathroom's size and use, its location within the house, and the number and style of fixtures to be included.

If you're remodeling an existing bath, you'll probably leave certain fixture locations undisturbed in the interest of economy. The toilet, for example, is usually best left where it is because of existing drain and vent lines, and there are obvious savings if the tub and lavatory are kept in the same general area (see the information on plumbing, pages 9-11).

However, if you're starting a new bathroom from scratch, keep an open mind about fixture placement. There are choices even where space is limited and small-scale fixtures can help you make the most of every square inch.

Minimum clearances

As a guideline, certain minimum distances between, to the side, and in front of fixtures have been established

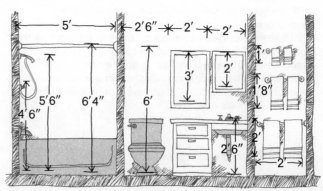

Use these *minimum measurements as a rough planning guide.*

and written into most building codes. These distances tell you how close together you can put the fixtures and still be able to use them comfortably and clean them easily. For example, if a lavatory is opposite a tub or toilet, 30 inches is a minimum clearance between them. Side-by-side fixtures, of course, can be located closer together.

Illustrated here are some examples of typical minimum clearances. Check with your local building department to find out exactly what guidelines are in effect in your community.

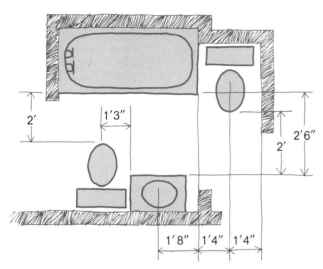

Typical minimum distances *for setting fixtures will help you in initial planning stages. But be sure to check exact local specifications before deciding on your floor plan and purchasing fixtures and materials.*

Deciding on a floor plan

Start by making cutouts to scale and, on graph paper scaled to the dimensions of your bathroom, move the fixtures around until you find the best arrangement. As you plan, be mindful of the range of fixture sizes and shapes available to you. Instead of a standard 5-foot-long bathtub, you may arrive at a better arrangement by using a 4-foot-square tub.

Position the tub before you plan the location of the other fixtures. Tub location is the first consideration simply because the tub takes up the greatest amount of space.

The basin, the most frequently used fixture, is usually best located out of the traffic zone. Because a basin with mirrors requires efficient illumination, it should be near a window to take advantage of the natural light.

If space permits, isolate the toilet with a partition or in a separate cubicle to create a sense of privacy (see compartmentalizing, pages 44–45). In any case, the toilet should be placed where it won't be visible from the doorway. If you are planning to include a bidet, it should be positioned adjacent to the toilet.

If you want to restrict the number of walls containing plumbing pipes (this usually saves money), you'll have fewer possibilities for fixture arrangements.

Basic bathroom floor plans

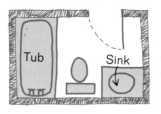

L-shaped plan, *most common design for smaller bathrooms, provides plenty of floor space, uses one wall of plumbing.*

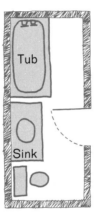

Bathroom on one wall *adapts to a long and narrow room— as narrow as 4½ feet. Here plumbing connections, drains, and vents are conveniently located along one wall.*

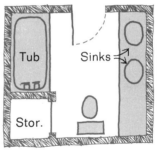

U-shaped plan *most practically utilizes space in a square room. Plumbing is more complicated, though, because it's divided and not confined to one wall.*

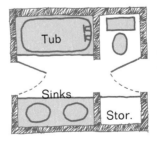

Corridor bath *can be small, could connect two bedrooms. It would be quite suitable for house with space for only one bathroom.*

What materials are best?

Smooth, easily cleaned, and nonabsorbent surfaces are most often recommended for bathrooms (and often required by codes). Your building inspector can tell you which materials, if any, are off limits.

Over a period of time, water affects almost any material it touches. Untreated wood in contact with water may change color; it may also warp, stain, or attract fungus growth. Stucco and concrete will streak, iron will rust, and copper will take on a greenish patina. Not all changes wrought by water are offensive, though; some materials acquire new dimension and beauty from their closeness to water.

Glass, marble, glazed tile, and laminated plastic are just about impervious to water except where there are joints, such as in the grouting between tiles or along fixture edges.

Costs

Bath materials—especially fixtures and fittings—are priced according to quality. More expensive fixtures last longer, look better, and function more efficiently. Economy fixtures from a reputable firm are likely to be well made, but they are usually less attractive than their costlier relatives.

Consider function and durability along with esthetic appeal and cost when you choose wall and floor materials, fixtures, and fittings. Ceramic tile, for example, is usually more expensive than other wall coverings, but it requires minimum maintenance. Basins with vanities, though costlier than wall-hung basins, offer extra storage space.

If you're stretching a budget, you're wise to purchase the best fixtures you can afford; they are permanent and cost no more to install than lower-quality materials. You can always upgrade floor and wall surfaces later on. You might also look into recycled materials such as old tubs and basins that can be reglazed; they can add character to a bath at a reasonable price. And don't overlook sales on fixtures and wall and floor materials.

Fixture materials

Most standard plumbing fixtures are made from porcelain-enameled stamped steel, porcelain-enameled cast iron, stainless steel, vitreous china, or fiberglass-reinforced plastic.

Enameled cast-iron fixtures weigh about three times as much as enameled steel fixtures, so they cost more to ship and handle. And they are a task to maneuver. But cast-iron fixtures—the world's standard since 1890—are durable, retain their glossy finish for years, resist chipping, and keep water hot.

Enameled steel is a blend of metals used for manufacturing strong but lightweight products. Less durable than cast iron because of a thinner coat of enamel, steel-based fixtures are frequently used for remodeling because they're easy to handle. Cleaned with non-abrasive products, they can last indefinitely.

Stainless steel, most often seen in the bath as a basin, is a durable material that resists discoloration as well as the effects of household chemicals. Stains from hard water and soap residue show up more on stainless steel than on porcelain enamel, so more frequent cleaning is required to keep stainless steel looking spotless.

Vitreous china is a carefully balanced mixture of clays that is poured into molds and dried. The resulting shape is sprayed with a glaze and fired in kilns. This attractive, easy-to-clean material is used for most toilets and bidets, and for many types of basins.

Fiberglass-reinforced plastic is molded at the factory into seamless, lightweight tubs and basins. It also appears often as one-piece tub and shower combinations with such features as grab bars, shower seats, arm rests, and soap niches. Available in a wide range of colors, these fixtures are warmer to the touch and easier to install than steel or iron, but they are usually less durable and require extra maintenance to retain their original finish.

Bathroom basins

Beautifully carved marble, gleaming metal, exotic giant clam shells, handcrafted pottery—any of these can be a suitable basin as long as it's the right shape, waterproof, and in accordance with local building codes. (See pages 52-53, for some striking basin treatments.)

Commercially available basins or sinks come in shapes and sizes to suit almost any building or remodeling plan. Yours can be rectangular, square, oval, round, triangular, or D-shaped. It can measure 11 by 11 inches, 19 by 16 inches, or 30 by 20 inches. Its back can be flat, slanted, or designed with a shelf ledge. A range of bright colors further widens the choice, and designs varying from simple bands of color to floral prints can coordinate your basin with your specific decorating scheme.

Standard heights from the floor to the sink rim range from 31 to 34 inches, though you can have the basin placed higher or lower to suit your height or personal preference. An 8-inch space between the top of the basin and the bottom of a mirror or medicine cabinet is recommended. For a countertop with an integral splashback, position the mirror at the top of the splash.

Examine actual basins available before you make a final choice on shape, size, color, and features such as shampoo spray attachments, lotion dispensers, and swing-away spouts.

Wall-hung basins

Brackets or hangers attached to the bathroom wall provide the main support for wall-hung basins, though they may have additional support from pedestals, legs, or storage cabinets below. Corner wall-hung basins can save space in a small bath.

If you replace one wall-hung sink with another, change

the bracket as well. If you plan to put a wall-hung sink in for the first time, you must tear out part of the wall directly behind the sink.

Supported *mainly by wall hangers, basin also rests on graceful pedestal.*

Countertop basins

Most basins are made to be supported by a counter, often with a cabinet underneath. Whatever counter or cabinet structure you choose, be sure to leave sufficient space around the pipes to permit repairs.

Styles. Usually countertop basins are either self-rimming with an integral lip that overlaps the counter opening to form a water seal (surface-mount), or they're recessed with a surrounding metal rim which provides the seal (flush-mount). Metal rims are available to match your hardware, so you don't need to settle for chrome if you have brass or gold-plated fittings.

Two other types of countertop sinks are available: under-the-counter basins and one-piece sink and counter units. Basins that fit underneath the countertop are a little difficult to keep clean, and they work best

with smooth counters of marble, synthetic marble, or plastic. Both basins have fittings mounted through the countertop instead of on the basin rim.

Double basins. Countertop basins are ideal where two basins are needed, since the basins can be joined by a continuous surface. Provide at least 12 inches—better yet 20 inches—between adjoining basin edges, and at least 6 to 8 inches between each basin and the side edge of the counter. For ample elbow room, you might situate basins at extreme ends of an L-shaped counter.

Fittings for fixtures

Fittings—faucets and handles—add the finishing touch to the plumbing fixtures installed in your new or remodeled bathroom, so they should be selected with care. Since tubs and basins are often sold without fittings, you are free to choose from chrome, acrylic, plastic, gold, or porcelain—whatever material suits your decorating plan and budget.

The price of fittings depends on the quality of brass used in their manufacture as well as the internal operating mechanism. Most fittings now available feature all-brass construction in basic parts. Generally, it's poor economy to buy cheap fittings, for the simple reason that they're likely to wear out quickly. It's also advisable to avoid off-brand or "bargain" fittings because of the difficulty in securing replacement parts later.

Basin fittings

Fittings for basins have either single-handle or double-handle controls. Decide which type of control you

Four countertop basins

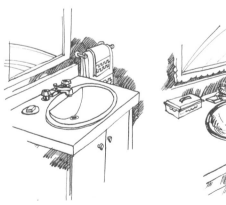

Surface-mounted

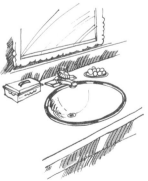

Flush-mounted

Recessed

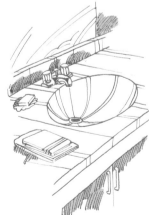

Integral

prefer and then make sure the mechanism will fit on the sink you've chosen. The number of holes in the sink and the distances between them tell you which fittings can be used with that sink. If you plan to attach fittings to a wall or counter, design the hole arrangement to suit the fittings.

If you're replacing basin fittings, a single-handle faucet will usually fit the present plumbing for single or double faucets. Before buying a new unit, though, measure the center-to-center distance between the holes in the basin where the faucet fits. Then ask for a new assembly with the same centers (usually 4, 6, or 8 inches).

Tub and shower fittings

Fittings for a bathtub include single or double-handle controls and a spout, sometimes with a built-in drain stop. Showers have a shower head and a control, and combination tub/showers have a tub spout, a shower head, a double or single-handle control, and a transfer valve that diverts water to the shower head. Some shower assemblies have shower heads at two different heights; others give a wide range of speed and direction of water. Most are equipped with water flow adjusters.

If you're replacing tub and shower faucets, the replacements must fit the faucet body behind the wall. (If the faucet assembly is an old one, you may have to replace the faucet body as well.) To be certain your new one will be the correct size, take the old faucet body with you to your supplier.

Choosing a toilet

Toilets (called "water closets" in building circles) vary in style, size, shape, installation, and mechanism. New colors brighten the selection, and toilets are more attractively designed and lower than they used to be.

In planning toilet placement, allow one inch between the toilet tank and the wall behind it, 15 inches to the center of the bowl from the side wall, and not less than 18 inches from the facing wall. If a toilet must face the door, allow room for the door to swing all the way open.

Replacing a noisy, old toilet with a newer model is relatively simple. Most floor-mounted toilets are designed to attach to standard fittings for water and waste piping, and though the installation procedure involves working with heavy, bulky objects in cramped space, it doesn't demand great plumbing skill.

Differences in flushing mechanism

Toilets commonly used for residences have a variety of flushing actions. These different actions result from bowl design and vary in noise generated, efficiency, and price.

Washdown toilets are the least expensive, least efficient, and most noisy. This type is most easily recognized by a characteristic bulge on the front exterior. It has a very small water surface inside the bowl, with a large, flat, exposed china surface at the front of the bowl interior. Since this area isn't protected by water, it's subject to staining and is difficult to clean. The washdown bowl is no longer accepted by many municipal code authorities.

Reverse trap action is efficient but moderately noisy. More of the interior surface is covered by water than in the washdown type.

Siphon jet is an improved version of the reverse trap—quieter and more efficient but also more expensive. Most of the exposed china surface is covered by water.

Siphon action mechanism is a refinement of the siphon jet. The toilet is a one-piece unit that's almost silent as it operates, leaves no dry surfaces, and is efficient and attractive. It's the most expensive.

Up-flush toilets are used in basements when the sewer is above basement floor level. They need no pipes below the basement floor. Instead, water enters through a double-acting flush valve. You purchase everything from the water-supply pipe to the sewage riser pipe as a package with the fixture; full plumbing and installation instructions come with the toilet.

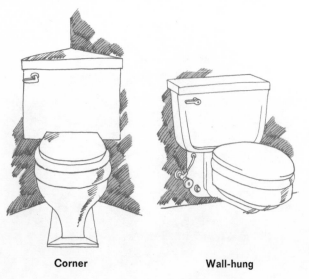

Three types of toilets

Some styles are quieter and easier to clean; most models are available in a wide variety of colors.

Corner   Wall-hung   Siphon jet

What styles are available?

In addition to differences in flushing mechanism, toilets have other features to choose from.

Water-saver toilets. Some toilet models are designed to make effective use of a low volume of water; they often utilize one-third less water than other toilets per use. A typical low-volume standard toilet requires only 3 gallons of water rather than the usual 5 to 7-gallon gulp. New state and federal energy conservation standards may specify a maximum 3-gallon-per-flush water use.

Wall-hung toilets. A good-looking, though expensive, alternative to the standard floor-mounted toilet is the wall-hung type. It makes floor cleaning easy. A wall-hung unit, however, must have a rather circuitous drainage layout, and it may clog more easily than floor-mounted toilets.

Installation of a wall-hung toilet calls for extensive modification of existing piping and alteration of the bathroom wall. This toilet requires a 6-inch wall for support (instead of the usual 4-inch wall), sometimes reinforced by a heavy L-brace that attaches to the floor. Since it expels waste through a wall connection, it requires the shifting of an existing soil pipe from its usual opening in the floor.

A special type of wall-hung toilet, the direct-flush model, is usually confined to commercial installations because it requires strong water pressure and is expensive to install, but since it has no working parts, it's easier to maintain.

Corner toilets. These toilets save space and are especially valuable in tiny half-baths. The tanks are triangular to fit precisely into a corner.

Elongated bowl toilets. Also called "extended rim toilets," these models are very attractive and easier to clean than round bowl designs. The extra inches create more comfortable seating and more water surface area. Municipal codes have required elongated bowls in commercial locations for many years. Now some cities are extending the requirement to apartment buildings.

Higher seat toilets. This type of toilet proves particularly useful for the aged or infirm. The rim of the bowl is 18 inches above the floor, in contrast to the 14-inch height of conventional bowls.

Accessories and options. If you foresee a problem with a sweating toilet tank, you can either purchase an internal drip guard or use an insulated tank. Devices are available that bring the water up to room temperature to prevent condensation—these either plug into an electric outlet or are installed beneath the tank. Some toilet models come with venting devices built into the flush mechanism.

Other extra touches are tank lids with integral planters, push-buttons instead of handles, and furniture-like frames that fit around standard toilets to make them look like chairs.

Lids, lid covers, and seats come in many materials, colors, and designs. Many of these lift off easily for cleaning.

A toilet paper holder may be decorative or merely functional, but it must be conveniently placed. The center of the toilet paper roll should be 26 inches from the floor; the edge of the roll should be 6 inches forward from the front of the bowl.

A magazine or book rack is another accessory to consider for the toilet area.

Bidets

If your bathroom has open floor area that could accommodate an additional fixture, consider installing a bidet. Used primarily for washing the perineal area, it is a sit-down wash basin provided with both hot and cold water and often a spray.

The usual location for a bidet is alongside the toilet. A bidet requires a minimum 3 by 3-foot floor area next to a wall. Installation can be quite expensive because of the need for both hot and cold-water connections and for a suitable drain. Fitting plumbing for a bidet into the existing piping involves opening walls and flooring.

Bidets come in colors to match the other fixtures. They're slightly lower than toilets in height.

Similar in design *to a sitz bath or a footbath, a bidet can substitute for them.*

Types of bathtubs

Many people feel that a luxurious bathtub is the item to splurge on when they plan a bathroom. Consequently, custom tubs of marble, tile, and wood are very popular. If you use reinforced concrete or fiberglass for a tub structure, almost any shape can be created.

But if you're on a budget, you'll be pleased to find that manufactured tubs are available in a widening range of sizes, colors, and shapes designed to meet specific requirements.

The substitution of a more modern tub for an old one can easily qualify as major home surgery rather than simple home improvement. This tends to be a big project for the weekend plumber because the task calls for know-how—and a clear track from the unloading site to the bathroom so that you can maneuver a heavy tub around corners, through doorways, and down hallways. Going up stairs is quite an undertaking.

To remove a built-in bathtub, you'll have to tear out the walls that enclose it. An enameled steel tub has a flange running along the sides to be fitted into a wall. Since a cast-iron tub has no flange, braces are needed between the studs.

To save on installation costs, choose a tub that will fit into the same space as the one it's replacing. Shorter, longer, and wider tubs often require changes in the house framing.

Having high sides, *this receptor (base) for a shower can serve as small bathtub. Receptor tubs usually have a corner seat, as do most square tubs.*

What kinds are available?

The most common tub, a rectangle 5 feet long by 30 inches wide, contributed to the predominance of 5-by-8-foot bathrooms. But new, more comfortable tub sizes are available, and new tub shapes and colors.

See page 22 for information about the materials tubs are made from. Typically, a standard tub made from enameled cast iron weighs from 350 to 500 pounds, an enameled steel tub weighs 100 to 250 pounds, and a fiberglass tub weighs 60 to 70 pounds.

Some bathtubs are designed with the drain in the angle formed by the end wall and floor rather than entirely on the floor of the tub. This type of fixture can be attached to drainpipes which run above the floor, as in concrete slab floor construction.

Standard rectangular tubs most often measure 5 feet long, 29 to 32 inches wide, and 16 inches high. This type of tub is readily available at most plumbing shops. Tubs in 4, 4½, 5½ and 6-foot lengths are generally available on special order. Some rectangular tubs have an oval-shaped or angled depression that provides the additional benefit of a built-in ledge for shampoo and soap. Larger rectangular tubs sometimes have a built-in seat on one side.

Most plumbing fixture makers offer standard rectangular tubs that can be installed flush with one, two, or three walls of the bathroom. The sides of the tub to be joined with walls have flanges which speed installation of finished wall materials and help prevent moisture from getting into the framing.

Modular tub/showers can replace both the tub and its enclosure. Often cast in one piece of fiberglass, these units are also available in a special kit for remodelers—this version comes in four pieces, neatly enclosed in two manageable cartons. For more information about showers, see pages 27-28.

Receptor tubs are low, squarish units, excellent for bathing children and doubling as the shower base for adults. Typical receptor tubs are 31 to 48 inches long, 42 to 49 inches wide, and 12 to 16 inches high. They can be set in a corner or recessed in a small alcove.

Square tubs fit nicely into corners. Some have seating niches at the corners. These range in size from a small 4-by-4-foot model to a capacious 5 by 5 feet. Square tubs have some disadvantages: they're difficult for elderly people to get into and out of, they demand a large volume of water, and they're awkward to clean.

Sunken tubs give an elegant effect. Standard sunken tubs come in varying shapes, sizes, and depths. Check the capacity of your water heater if you're planning a sunken tub of larger-than-normal size.

A sunken tub can be installed as part of a remodeling project if there's room under the floor to accommodate it. This space may be provided by the crawl area beneath the first floor, a garage under a second-story bathroom, or even a stairwell. Extra framing is often necessary to carry the weight of a sunken tub built on the second story.

Before installing a sunken tub, consider the safety hazards involved. Sunken tubs can cause accidents in households with small children or elderly residents. The potential hazard can usually be reduced by careful design which treats the sunken tub as a separate entity, like a miniature indoor swimming pool. Handy grab bars are highly desirable.

Oversize tubs large enough to hold two adults are also available from your plumbing supply dealer. These require substantial support framing and a back-up water heater, and you should make sure the one you want can be brought into your house through existing doorways.

Built-in *recessed inlets direct swirling water into whirlpool tub; portable whirlpool units are also available.*

Whirlpool tubs with built-in hydromassage units are costly because of the jet-pump mechanism and the extensive changes in piping and wiring needed for their installation. But for those who enjoy this exhilarating type of tub bath, the extra expense may be worth it. These tubs are available in various materials in square and rectangular shapes, sunken and oversize models.

Japanese tubs *(furos)* are available in fiberglass and, in some areas, traditional wood. This tub is a deep well that accommodates one or more soakers seated in steaming water up to the chin. Such a tub may require space under the floor to accommodate the extra depth and is probably best installed at ground level. It also may need an extra-capacity water heater or a supplementary heater of its own. (See pages 70–71.)

Safety and convenience features

Check for nonslip texture in the bottom surface of any tub that you wish to purchase. Texturing is particularly desirable if the tub is to be used as a shower also. Some new models have a mildly roughened surface that's too subtle to emboss the anatomy of a person sitting in the tub, yet rough enough to discourage a foot from skidding. This style has replaced the patterned tub bottoms popular a few years ago, which have proved difficult to keep clean and less skid-resistant than originally thought. (Avoid the temptation to add stick-on skid pads in the tub. These wear off in time, provide little actual skid resistance, and offer a refuge for dirt and bacteria.)

Tubs with built-in lumbar supports are more comfortable than those with all sides vertical. Headrests and armrests are also available. Grab bars built into the sides of tubs are becoming more common, especially on large rectangular tubs. Though drains are usually placed under the faucets, you can get tubs with drains positioned elsewhere. A drain at the opposite end of the tub from the faucets makes tub cleaning easier.

You can determine the water depth of a bathtub by measuring the distance from the overflow to the bottom drain. A foot of water in the tub is needed for a good soaking.

Around the tub you'll need places for sponges, soap, shampoo, bath oils, and brushes; a rack to hang towels and washcloths; and a spot to store towels.

Showers and tub/showers

Shower stalls can be fabricated during construction of a new bathroom, or they can be purchased in prefabricated form—various manufacturers produce them. A shower can be in combination with a bathtub, in a separate stall or compartment, or in a portion of the bathroom that has undergone waterproofing and drain installation for use as a doorless shower area.

Showers can be purchased or constructed in a variety of sizes, but for comfort, a shower stall should be at least 3 feet square.

The most economical way to provide a shower is to add a shower head to an existing bathtub. The two ways to convert a tub to a tub/shower are to build a spray head into the wall above the tub or to add a movable spray head on a flexible cable. If permanent shower fittings are installed, the pipes for the shower are usually concealed in the wall. A movable shower head can be added without changing the plumbing; it's likely to use less water than a regular shower, and it's useful for cleaning the tub.

Shower and tub/shower enclosure materials

The wall surfaces around any type of shower must be finished in a moisture-resistant material. Plastic laminates, ceramic tile, cultured marble, and fiberglass-reinforced plastic are some of the materials that can be used. It's important that this wall surface be installed properly

Tiled, sunken tub/shower has convex skylight that allows standup head room. Architect: Ed Heine.

because considerable damage can result if the joints aren't water resistant.

Some manufacturers of bathtub and shower combinations solve the watertight installation problem by making shower walls of fiberglass-reinforced plastic integral with a fiberglass shower base or tub. The entire unit is installed as one fixture.

Other tub/shower surrounds are made in three sections that fit around the top of the bathtub. The sheets are sealed to each other and to the top of the tub so that water can't leak through to the wall. Laminated hardboard or melamine-laminated plywood panels designed expressly as tub enclosures can be attached directly to the studs or applied over gypsum wallboard. Most cities require that gypsum wallboard behind a tub or shower be a special water-resistant type.

Manufactured showers

Standard showers are constructed of fiberglass-reinforced plastic or of metal.

Lightweight molded fiberglass showers and tub/showers have a smooth surface with rounded corners for easy cleaning and can be quickly set in place and attached to framing members. The shower stalls are available in two styles. One is a complete stall—floor, three walls, and optional ceiling—molded as a single, large unit. The other, designed for remodeling projects, is formed of four basic components that are glued together on the site. The drain mechanism is usually part of the package. Fiberglass units come in a choice of colors; sizes and heights vary. They often have soap dishes, ledges, towel racks, and seats molded into the structure during manufacture.

Integral *tub/shower and wall surround made of seamless fiberglass can come with molded-in soap dishes, ledges, niches, or a seat.*

However, there are some possible problems. If a combination shower and shower enclosure comes in one piece—especially if it's a tub/shower—the unit might not pass through narrow hallways or through the bathroom door. Fiberglass will scratch if you clean it with abrasive cleaners. Precisely tailored framing is required to give fiberglass units firm surrounding support and to make sure that their rectangular box form will fit into an irregular space without flexing when in use.

If a fiberglass unit appeals to you, shop for it carefully. Some of the first-generation models were flimsy, and a few may still be on the market. Arrange with the plumbing supply dealer to show you the latest models in his warehouse or stock room. Examine construction features carefully before investing. A high-quality product, made by a reputable firm and properly installed, will give trouble-free service indefinitely. The latest models are more resistant to scuffing and chemical stains (except nicotine) than some of the earlier ones. The fiberglass is coated with a protective gel sealant that wears off in time. You can postpone this dulling by cleaning with liquid cleansers instead of abrasive powders. The original surface can be restored by the company that installs the fiberglass unit.

Metal showers are also available. Tin is very inexpensive but extremely noisy, and tin shower stalls vibrate. Cheaper metals can rust. Stainless steel showers are more expensive and attractive, but they water spot.

Custom showers

Custom showers are generally more expensive than standard ones, but in some cases they're the only kind that will fit into the bathroom design the homeowner has in mind. Ceramic tile is used for most custom showers, but other waterproof surfacing materials can be used. Careful attention must be given to waterproofing joints.

Tiled showers are relatively expensive and the joints can be difficult to clean, but silicone grouts are said to discourage mildew growth. Tile can be applied with mastic over gypsum wallboard or plaster, or it can be set into wet mortar. Pregrouted tile shower surrounds are available in sizes to fit the most popular receptors. They consist of several pregrouted sheets and internal corner strips. Limited on-site grouting and cuts are required.

The floor of a custom shower is usually either a purchased waterproof receptor, available in a range of colors, types, and sizes, or a fabricated receptor of ceramic tile or some other suitable material. The standard prefabricated receptors come in set dimensions. A custom-built shower base requires the installation of a shower pan made of sheet lead or copper or a waterproof and damp-proof membrane formed to the desired size and shape. The membrane, frequently a lamination of heavy paper and asphalt reinforced with glass fibers, costs considerably less than sheet lead or copper.

When planning a custom shower, consult a contractor or plumber to make sure that construction will conform with local building and sanitation codes.

Accessories for safety, convenience

Look into a number of ways to make your shower safer. To prevent falls, install a vertical grab bar, making sure screws attach it through the wall into the studs. Make certain the shower door operates easily and won't break. Any light fixture used above a shower should be vaporproof. An exhaust fan will aid in removing moisture and vapor. The base of the shower should have a nonskid surface.

Thermal mixing valves make it easier to get the desired water temperature. Other fixtures allow you to dial the temperature you want.

The shower head should be installed high enough to ensure head clearance for adults. A storage shelf approximately 40 inches above the shower floor is convenient. All shower surfaces, including any seat or shelf, should be self draining.

The choice in floor finishes

Since bathroom floors are subjected to water and moisture, they should be surfaced with materials that resist water. Resilient flooring (in tile or sheet form), carpeting, and ceramic tile are the most commonly used flooring materials in bathrooms. Other possibilities include polyurethaned stenciled, painted, or natural wood, poured floors, or marble floors. Wood floors may need to be refinished periodically with a water-resistant seal or varnish. Rugs are often used in bathrooms as accents. To make concrete floors more attractive, consider adding color to the cement mixture at the time of construction or painting the finished floor with one of the special concrete floor paints.

No one floor finish has all the properties desirable in a bathroom floor. The flooring decision may depend on your skill in installation if you plan to do the job yourself. Many of the troubles that develop with bathroom floor finishes can be attributed to poor installation. Other considerations include durability of the floor finish, its cost, ease of upkeep, resistance to soil and indentation, and quietness.

Light or neutral flooring colors offer the most flexibility in decorating and make small bathrooms appear larger than dark or patterned floors do. Select materials in colors that you won't tire of quickly.

How to carpet a bathroom

Repair the floor if it's worn (especially if it has wide cracks or depressions) and remove the bathroom door. Be careful not to disturb plumbing connections. Make a pattern from heavy paper, as shown in photo sequence. Spread carpeting, face down, on a bare floor. Piece as necessary and lay pattern *also face down* on carpeting. If possible, position the pattern so a bound edge of carpeting will fall along the door sill. Tape pattern to carpeting. When you can, cut between rows of tufting to avoid cutting the stitches.

You'll need *squares of heavy paper, cellophane tape, masking tape, and scissors; possibly a pencil, measuring tape, and razor blades.*

Starting in corner, *make pattern of floor by taping squares of heavy paper together, letting them overlap each other by ½ inch.*

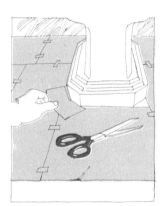

Keeping edges snug, *fit pattern around fixtures and indentations for door jamb molding. Cover floor; leave slit from back of each fixture to the wall. Remove pattern.*

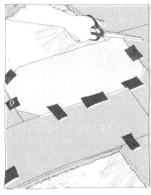

Place pattern face down *on the back of the carpet and tape it to carpet securely. Cut slits for fixtures as the pattern indicates; then cut out the openings for the fixtures.*

Seam carpet *by laying sections side by side, taping them together with masking tape or a pressure sensitive tape. You'll have to repeat the process after each laundering.*

Finished carpet *is soft and warm underfoot. The heavier the carpet, the smoother it will be. Because of splashing in children's baths, avoid carpeting unless floor is heated.*

Carpeting in a bathroom

Carpeting under bare feet is great on cold winter mornings. Besides contributing warmth, carpeting can prevent slips and falls; and a bottle or glass dropped on a carpeted floor will probably bounce rather than break. Soft carpeting is quieter than hard flooring materials.

It's advisable to use washable carpeting, such as nylon, loose laid so it can be removed periodically for cleaning. Some synthetic fibers retard water absorption; some carpeting is treated with mildew, stain, and odor-resistant substances. Tweeds and patterns don't show soil as fast as solid colors.

If you anticipate needing extra resistance to stain and wear, kitchen carpeting is a practical choice. Indoor-outdoor carpeting is another durable possibility, though it tends to retain water. Inexpensive carpeting is available at special remnant sales and at overrun outlets.

Some backing materials, such as vinyl foam, stand up well to moisture. Carpeting with a backing is more comfortable to stand on, especially for a first-floor bathroom on a concrete slab.

Even though you intend to install carpeting, the floor underneath should be in good condition; otherwise, moisture soaking through the carpeting may cause permanent damage to the floor support structure. Worn floors may be hidden successfully by carpeting, but they shouldn't be worn to such an extent that they no longer protect the subflooring.

Using ceramic tile

Matte or crystalline glazed ceramic tile is more durable than highly glazed wall tile, which is usually not used on the floor. (But there are always exceptions: the beauty of highly glazed tile may outweigh more practical considerations.) Unglazed mosaic tile makes a very durable floor, as does quarry tile. Shapes of floor tiles include hexagons, octagons, rectangles, large or small squares, and Spanish or Moorish patterns. Tile surfaces can be smooth, abrasive nonslip, or carved.

Tiles of hardened impervious glass are also available in a broad range of shapes and colors for use on floors or walls. Cement grout is suggested for glass tiles.

Most tile companies manufacture floor tile which harmonizes with the colors of their wall tile. If you want a blend of tile colors, you can order different percentages of each shade. Varying tile textures, shapes, and colors can be combined for individual effects. Tile manufacturers often stock a selection of popular blends and multicolor patterns.

Colored grout can be used as a design element. When contrasting grout is used, special precautions must be taken to seal the tile before the grout is applied.

Floor tiles can be installed over concrete, plywood, wood, or hardboard, at grade or above grade level. Pre-grouted sheets of tile save installation time. Smooth-surfaced polyurethane grout resists stains, mildew, bacteria, and chemical corrosion, and it's flexible enough to move as the house structure settles. Because water eventually seeps through the grout (though it won't penetrate the tiles themselves) the backing must be durable and not affected by water.

Be sure to purchase and save extra tiles for possible future repairs and replacements. Patterns and glazes change, and often it's impossible to match colors a few years after the initial installation.

Resilient flooring

If you plan to install resilient flooring in your bathroom, you can just about expect to spend the afternoon in the store that supplies it. This is an economical and popular material, and the choices in designs, colors, and textures are rife.

Made from vinyl asbestos, solid vinyl, or vinyl-cork, resilient flooring is manufactured either in sheets up to 12 feet wide (preferred for use in bathrooms because it requires fewer seams and thus gives better resistance to moisture) or in 9-inch, 12-inch, and 16-inch tiles. You'll find both sheets and tiles in hundreds of their own designs—many embossed with a grained, pitted, or fissured surface—as well as in very good imitations of rough-textured brick, smooth marble, wood parquet, tile, slate, and other natural materials.

Vinyl-asbestos, the most popular resilient flooring in use today, has a durable, nonporous surface that resists moisture, dirt, wear, and indentation. Many brands have an easy-maintenance "no wax" surface. Tiles often come in easy-installation self-stick backings: all you do is peel off the paper backing, press the tile in place, and walk on it.

Solid vinyl has the same advantages as vinyl asbestos, though it's generally more expensive because of its brighter colors and gloss.

Variations include cork tile, which is naturally resilient and made durable with a tough vinyl coating; and materials such as fabric, hardwood veneers, and marble chips that are either suspended in solid vinyl or laminated between a base and a vinyl wearing surface.

Finishes for the walls and ceiling

Many of the same materials are used on both bathroom walls and ceilings. A few materials, such as acoustical tile, are usually confined to ceiling use. The ceiling should be completed before the walls are decorated. Walls around showers and tubs must meet specific moisture-resistance requirements (see page 27).

The other bathroom walls should be reasonably protected from moisture damage. This protection is more critical in small, enclosed bathrooms where humidity builds up quickly than in larger, more open bathrooms. Check local codes for any restrictions on the type of bathroom wall finish you can use. Water-resistant wall materials include ceramic tile, mirrors, vinyl products, plastic-finished or laminated hardboards, and marble. Other wall materials used in bathrooms include wood with protective finishes, painted plaster or gypsum wallboard, and vinyl-protected wallcoverings.

The color, pattern, and texture of the wall surface has a strong effect on the overall color scheme and decorative effect of a bathroom since the walls make up a large percentage of the room area. A prominent pattern on the walls will overshadow the other features of the bathroom; choose accessories accordingly to avoid a clash of patterns or styles. If you can't find a wall finish to match the fixture colors exactly, it's better to use contrasting colors on the walls.

Using wallpapers and fabrics

Wallpapers, fabrics, and vinyl wallcoverings come in many colors and designs. They're often available with matching fabrics that you can use for curtains or a shower curtain.

Vinyl-laminated, vinyl-coated and plastic-coated wallpapers are washable and scrubbable and will stand up well under humidity. Vinyl-coated fabric is also available in many different patterns and colors. You could apply a waterproofer over standard fabric or paper.

Wallpapering a small bathroom is relatively inexpensive. If the room is large, try papering one wall.

Prepasted and pretrimmed papers make it easier to do the work yourself; strippable papers make changes easier. Check to be sure that the adhesive is moisture-proof.

Paint in the bathroom

Paint is an inexpensive, easy-to-apply bathroom wall finish. Paint used on bathroom walls should be moisture

and mildew resistant and easy to clean. Alkyds (oil-based) paints should be used on bath walls and ceilings—these paints are both durable and washable. The higher the gloss, the smoother the finish and, consequently, the easier it is to clean. Gloss or semi-gloss enamel is commonly recommended for bathrooms.

Paint can be custom mixed to match fixtures and other items exactly.

Ceramic and plastic tile for walls

Ceramic tiles have traditionally been the first choice for bathroom walls. Wall tiles vary from 1-by-1-inch squares to huge Spanish shapes measuring 9½ inches from tip to tip. The most frequently used wall tile measures 4½ by 4½ inches. Wall tiles often have a bright, shiny glaze. When decorated tile is used, it becomes a very important design element.

For more information on using ceramic tile, see page 30.

Plastic wall tile is inexpensive and comparatively easy for a home workman to install. Like ceramic tile, plastic tile is available in many colors.

Rigid wall panels

Most wall panels can be installed quickly and easily; just be sure they'll fit through the doorway. The expanding range of paneling colors and patterns makes for interesting decorating possibilities.

Sheet vinyl for bathroom use comes with a moisture-resistant backing; some brands of plastic laminates, familiar as counter coverings, are available also for use on bathroom walls. Some plastic laminate panels have a polystyrene core that compensates for subwall irregularities. Plastic-coated hardboards wipe clean easily.

Decking (above) salvaged from old ship covers shower walls; tiles line tub base. Outside entrance lets swimmers in to share double-size tub/shower without crossing carpet.
Etched porthole (right) near shower displays walrus.

Ship's linen closet converts to bath vanity. Marble facing from razed building covers top of counter.

Counter possibilities

Counters next to a sink should be water resistant; they needn't be waterproof if you wipe off splashes right away. But check your local codes to see if they restrict counter materials.

The range of materials that can be used as counter-tops is wide. Counters can be made of the same material as the walls or the floor. If there's cabinetry under the counter, the color and type of counter material should cabinets. Counters containing an integral sink are available in several materials, such as laminated plastic and simulated marble, in a choice of sizes and shapes.

Ceramic tile, plastic laminate, and plastic-coated hardboard are the most common bathroom counter materials. Simulated marble is also very popular. With tile, initial installation is expensive, but tile is more durable than most other surfaces. Plastic laminate is easy to clean and inexpensive to install. Counters can also be made of polyurethaned wood, metal, or marble (listed from least to most expensive).

Splashing bathrooms

- **Bathrooms before and after**
- **Elegant master baths, efficient family baths**
- **Special tubs and basins**
- **Bathroom spas and saunas**
- **The energy-efficient bath**
- **Garden baths**

Sometimes it's hard to imagine that the most personal —and next to the kitchen, the most often remodeled— room in your house is the same room that once was the destination of that fast trip across the back yard on a dark and stormy night. And even in the era of the early built-in bath, it still translated into little more than a homely, tiled cubicle.

Today, thanks to multicolored fixtures, fiberglass spas, sun lamps, Finnish saunas, and the imagination of talented architects and designers, bathrooms have come into their own as rooms that allow you all the joys of a long, tranquil soak in an oversize tub, all the esthetic pleasure of showering in view of, or among, exterior and interior gardens, and all the efficiency and comfort even Queen Victoria might envy were she alive today.

On the following pages you'll find a sparkling collection of contemporary bathrooms, some of whose features may fit perfectly into your own building or remodeling scheme. To illustrate how dramatic an effect a little remodeling and redecorating can produce in the bath, we start off with a collection of before-and-after photographs of some wonderful bathrooms transformed from cramped, gloomy, or poorly planned spaces.

Further on you'll find some elegant ideas for master baths (pages 40–43) and bathroom spas (pages 68–69), a delightful glass block shower (page 48), marvelous directions to take with bathroom basins (pages 52–53), a bathroom shelving system to build (page 55), and tips for using color when you decorate (page 63).

Consider, too, the energy-saving ideas presented on pages 72–73 and the safety suggestions on page 75. Both energy conservation and bathroom safety are areas of very practical concern to bathroom planners.

As you browse through these ideas, observe how color, materials, and fixtures are blended to create a unified atmosphere. Try to keep that goal in mind as you plan the bath you want.

Pine and tile pullman *invites an epicurean soak in the tile spa, or perhaps simply a shower with the greenhouse garden in view. Dramatically transformed from a small, cramped bath when the owners went beyond the house foundation to install the tub/spa, the new bath now has plenty of room plus generous storage (see page 60). Architect: James K. Bell.*

BATHROOMS ...BEFORE AND AFTER

Before: *Typical of its era, the 7½ by 10-foot, 1936 bath had only one place in which to put things—a wall-hung medicine cabinet.*

Now the side yard enhances bathroom

This remodeled bathroom takes advantage of a narrow side yard instead of hiding it as before. Vines traveling up fishline outside the windows and the pale amber glass combine to ensure privacy.

The standard tub, sheathed with wood, incorporates an open planter box at one end to hold potted plants.
Architect: Mark Mills.

Redesigned, rebuilt by the owners

The range of light and dark tones in the wood used for walls and cabinets adds surface interest. Dark grout contrasts with large white tile squares on the counter and the splashback. White-painted, rough-feeling adobe tub walls introduce another natural texture.

This bathroom exchanged space with the adjoining kitchen. The kitchen now is larger; the bathroom is still a comfortable size and efficient.

The owners did the plumbing, wiring, and tile work themselves.

Plans: Sink was moved and set in an alcove, and bathroom entrance was moved. Soil stack stayed in same place.

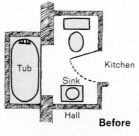

Before

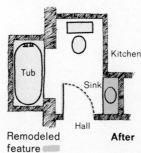

Remodeled feature

After

Soffit light *over basin supplements ceiling fixtures. Wooden towel racks and paper holder were designed, built by the owner.*

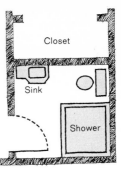

Before

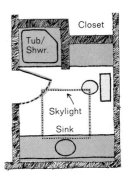

After

◢ Remodeled feature

Plans: *To expand and modernize bathroom, adjacent bedroom closet was added.*

Twin arches *that blend with the architecture of the rest of the house fill one wall. Adjustable glass shelves in the second arch allow light to reach plants.*

Handy, pull-out cabinet *has two plastic bin inserts: one is used as a laundry hamper, the other as a waste basket. Butcher block makes an attractive counter.*

Attractive, practical for adults, children

In its new form, this remodeled 1946 bathroom fills the needs of parents, child, and guests. The shower base is a receptor tub, deep enough to bathe a child in. Storage includes locked drawers, portable baskets, and a pull-out cabinet.

A blue and white-patterned tile used for the floor and for detailing accents the cool blue and white color scheme. Natural light enters the bathroom through a square skylight that's fitted with two frosted bulbs for night illumination.

Architect: Michael D. Moyer.

Now: *Window is covered up and ceiling opened with large skylight. On the left are a standard tub and shower stall.*

Before: *Inconvenient bathroom had dinky window, improvised storage.*

Adding skylight opens bath to the sky

A 4 by 6-foot skylight brightens and opens up a remodeled bathroom. The skylight exterior can be hosed down from the roof; the inside is cleaned by hand.

This bath is in an 1897 house that had already been remodeled once when the "before" photograph was taken. Fixtures projected into the room, the light level was low, and storage space was inadequate.

The new cabinets are made of overlaid plywood that was oiled, sealed with polyurethane, and trimmed with walnut. Cabinets house a sink, roll-out hamper, cupboards, and 10 drawers.

Architect: Bruce Wendell Beebe.

Paper, paint create new sophistication

With a minimum of structural change, the bathroom acquired an entirely fresh, new look. First, a projecting wall was removed. Then modern fixtures replaced the old ones, a round skylight was added, the walls were papered in a striking black and white geometric pattern, and a plush red carpet was installed.

Because the owner is tall, the new countertop measures 40 inches high (usual height is 36 inches) and the shower/tub enclosure is oversize.

Inside the bathroom, white built-in cabinets and drawers provide plenty of storage; there's even a hamper built into one wall. Row lights on both sides of the wood-framed mirror supplement the skylight, which includes rheostatted electric lights.

Architect: George Cody. Interior Designer: Stewart Morton.

Before: *Awkward partition was in the way in old-fashioned bathroom.*
View past *floor-to-ceiling drawers into bath shows new basin area. The mirror on 6-inch projection gives person shaving a close view.*

Display places for plants add life, color

After choosing honey-colored oak for its light and airy effect, the owners of this bathroom decided on tile in a light shade to enhance and harmonize with the wood rather than a dark or bold-patterned tile that would overwhelm it. One continuous wall is finished with tongue-and-groove oak flooring treated with sealer and polyurethane. White cabinetry and fixtures also complement the wood; growing plants provide texture and focal points.

Plants live under slightly different growing conditions in the lavatory area and in the shower room. The planter behind the basin has the advantages of direct sunlight and watering convenience. The tub/shower area tends to have a variable high humidity level, warmer air temperature, and reflected light. The owners rotate pots of flowering plants and experiment with exotics difficult to grow elsewhere in the house.

Architect: Michael D. Moyer.

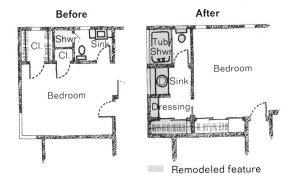

Before **After**

Remodeled feature

Plans: *More usable than before, master bath and bedroom were remodeled without exterior construction. Moving the plumbing and rearranging walls added elbow room; spaces for plants were incorporated into the design. A total of four rooms (bedroom, dressing room, lavatory area, and tub/toilet compartment) now work smoothly together as a unit.*

Sunken tub/shower *saves space, works well for both showers and baths. It's slightly larger than usual, measuring 3 by 6 feet. The top shelf was designed specifically for plants; the lower shelf—for storing odds and ends—slopes slightly for drainage. Shelves against the window hold more potted plants.*

Suspended mirror *"floats" between basin and built-in, metal-lined planter that has drainage holes to outside.*

Accessories *include a streamlined magazine holder built into the new wall.*

BATHROOMS ...BEFORE AND AFTER

1868 tub in a linear bathroom

A shallow lot line directed the design here. The solution to the narrow site was to string out compartments in a linear fashion, creating separate spaces that can be used with privacy.

Duckboard floor sections in both tub and sauna compartments have drains beneath to carry off water. The bay beside the tub allows room for a convenient ledge; the leaded glass window is set at an angle to provide privacy and bring light down to the tub.

Architect: Richard Ehrenberger.

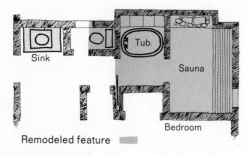

Remodeled feature ▪

Plans: *Toilet compartment, part of the original house, was rotated 90°. Then new compartments for the tub and for the sauna were added on.*

Little girl *plays with movable shower head (also useful for shampooing and for rinsing the tub). The 1868 tub, designed to conserve space in a maid's room, is deep but only 3½ feet long.*

Now bathroom fills its owners' needs

Remodeled for two working adults, this bathroom is now extremely functional, as well as attractive. It's divided into three activity zones: a corner of washbasins and cabinets; a compartment for the toilet; and a glass-walled enclosure containing a double shower.

The sink area was formerly a closet for the master bedroom; adding this space to the bathroom doubled its size. As part of extensive remodeling, the entire house was replumbed. Separate plumbing lines provide variable temperature and water pressure for each shower head.

The cabinets were designed by Greg Smith, The Just Plain Smith Company.

Before: *Walled off from the house's side yard, bathroom appears small and stuffy.*

Spacious shower enclosure *that replaced a tub looks out to garden through new window wall.*

Two higher-than-usual *antique basins inset in marble countertop sections double efficiency, save time. Collection of mirrors and pictures personalizes the wall above the basins. Gold fixtures and oak cabinets add color and texture.*

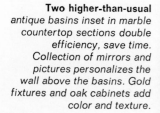

Great old tub *with feet was refinished, painted. The enlarged window above it changed the character of the bathroom by giving a new impression of space and movement. From the tub, there's a delightful view to a hillside garden. The slope of the hill and the trees provide privacy.*

New windows *have small panes to match the ones elsewhere in the house; the owner had them made to his specifications and installed them himself. The basin inset in the marble countertop is new.*

Doing their own work and recycling cut costs

A year of searching led to the discovery of this antique French cabinet; the owners planned their bathroom remodeling project around it. They had decided that standard cabinets were dull but that building their own was too expensive. Since the existing bathroom was too small for the cabinet, they pushed a wall out 18 inches to create a cabinet alcove.

After consulting an architect, the owners gutted, rewired, replumbed, and rebuilt the room themselves. It took them about a month of weekends and after-work hours to rip out and do the basics; then it required two months to put the new room together.

Walls, floor, and shower enclosure are built of redwood tongue-and-groove boards (a square-jointed milling so the grooves between the boards meet instead of making a "V"). Six coats of polyurethane sealer and five coats of satin polyurethane protect the wood surfaces.

Architect: James Bell.

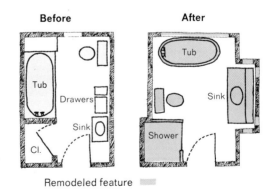

Remodeled feature ▬

Plans: *Built 50 years ago, bathroom in summer home that became a permanent residence had been remodeled in the early 1950s. To relieve the '50s look, fixtures were moved around and important new windows added. Part of an adjoining closet was incorporated into a new shower stall.*

Plan: *Converted from a spare bedroom, new master bath is reached through a large open doorway. Tub is in a large bay window; shower and toilet have their own compartments.*

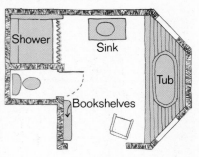

Shower

Sink

Tub

Bookshelves

Draw back *the pretty pleated drape to reach the shower. Shower stall and adjacent toilet compartment have their own overhead lights; wall lamps and windows light the rest of the room.*

Camouflaged fixtures—*and shelves stacked with Agatha Christie mysteries—make this Victorian master bath more like a sitting room. The basin was built into an antique cabinet, the tub into a window seat, and toilet and shower were compartmented behind a closet door and drape.*

From extra bedroom to elegant bath

When is a bath not a bath? When it's so elegant you can use it for a dining room…which, with the addition of table and settings, is exactly what owners of this one have done when they've hosted large dinner parties. Converted from a spare bedroom in a grand old Victorian house, the bath seems more like an extension of the master bedroom because fixtures are camouflaged in an antique cabinet and window seat, or hidden in compartments behind a curtain and door.
     Architect: Herbert D. Kosovitz.

Elegant fixtures *personalize a master bath whose ancestors—two small, 20-year-old baths—were cramped and inadequate. The remodeled bath has twin basins, circular shower, and bidet.*

A show of spectacular fixtures

Imported Italian fixtures became the focal point when homeowners threw out two small back-to-back bathrooms to make way for a new master bath. Elegantly sculptured pedestal basins stand below his-and-hers mirrored cabinets; toilet and bidet are on the other side of a compact, revolving storage unit. Owners put down the teak parquet floor themselves and finished it with several coats of protective polyurethane.

Preplumbed *circular shower was tucked into one corner of the bathroom, in view of a private deck and teakwood hot tub.*

Ideas for master bathrooms

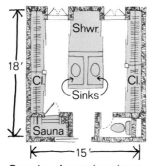

Oversize shower *has doors to his-and-hers dressing areas. Architect: Noyola & Abels.*

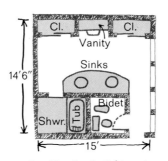

Combination *bath/dressing room contains two closets.*

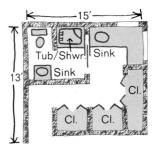

Dressing area *connects bath with master bedroom.*

MASTER BATHS: TWO ROUTES TO CHARACTER

Plan: *Cantilevering the tub out over the roof widened a narrow second-story bath and gave it a garden view.*

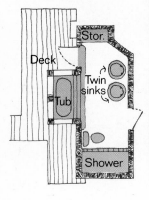

Cantilevered bay *frames a tub that was uprooted from a dark alcove and moved to a spot with a garden view as part of a major remodeling project. In order to expand their bath, owners knocked a hole in an outside wall and put the tub over the lower-level roof; then they added a second-story deck that's reached through a door in the new bath.*

Twin pedestal basins *are antiques; one was already in the bath, the other was uncovered in a recycled fixtures shop.*

Second-story bath has a cantilevered tub

Knocking out a wall to expand a bathroom is often a foregone conclusion when the problem is a too-small space, particularly at ground level. But what do you do when the small bath belongs to an upstairs master bedroom? You can cut into part of an adjoining room, though you could be left with a rob-Peter-to-pay-Paul situation. Or, as these owners did, you might still be able to open a wall and go out.

What owners called a "skinny little nasty bath" before they bumped out an outside wall and cantilevered the tub over the roof below is now a spacious and functional section of the master suite. Framed by a handsome bay window, the tub area looks out onto a second-story deck that also was built when the bath was remodeled.

Interior Designer: Michael Vincent.

Framed with cobalt blue tile, *a partly sunken tub and a glass-enclosed shower share the same wall. Continuity between the square-blue and white tiles on walls and ledge and the hexagonal tiles on floor is achieved with gray grout.*

Ceiling mirrors *are the medium for bringing light into a master bath that was created when howeowners moved their master suite into the attic. Fitted neatly into a ceiling well, the mirrors reflect light from a small window over the basin. Along the wall, a band of wood pegs is for towels and robes; bench sections lift on hinges for access to storage below. Adjacent dressing room is equipped with a ballet bar for exercise.*

Bathroom done in a play on light

Without the imaginative use of mirrors, this crisp-looking master bath might look more like the shadowy attic from which it was transformed than the sparkling room it is. The mirrors, framed in modules into a ceiling well, catch light that comes into the room through a dormer window above the basin and then throw it back throughout the bath. And though it's indirect, additional light comes from a wall of mirrors, a window, and a skylight in the neighboring dressing/exercise room.

In order to maintain as great a feeling of spaciousness as is possible in a small bathroom under a sharply pitched roof line, the architect painted or tiled the walls white, installed a clear glass shower stall, and dropped the tub a little below floor level.

Architect: Jennifer Clements.

Plan: *Master bath, linked to dressing area by pocket door, has tub and shower along one wall, storage along the other.*

THE FAMILY BATH: MAKING ROOMS OF VANITY, TUB, AND TOILET

Two-room bath for the kids

If you want to make one bathroom serve two or more people at once, consider breaking it up into two or more compartments. Compartmentalizing is both an efficient and an economical means of making the best use of limited facilities.

Here, for instance, in the inner room of the bath they share, Jonah can tack his toy boat through bathtub straits while Alicia, in the outer compartment, brushes her hair for school. Lighting for the fully mirrored vanity is achieved with clear glass globes on a dimmer.

Architect: Fisher/Friedman Associates.

Compartmentalized bath *separates vanity and basin from tub and toilet with a ceiling-high door. To keep things simple, kids store toothbrushes and bathroom toys in vanity drawers, stash dirty clothes in a pull-out hamper. Chrome towel bars are the sturdy industrial type.*

Recessed shelves *by the tub store odds and ends; low window lets little ones look out, too. Accordion-fold shower door stacks neatly against the wall.*

Variations for family baths

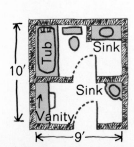

Outer area *allows for quick hair combing and hand washing; inner room contains rest of fixtures.*

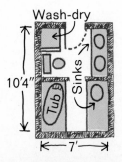

Useful additions *include a drip-dry compartment and extra counter space for baby care.*

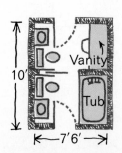

Separate doors *lead into double bath having a convenient dressing table.*

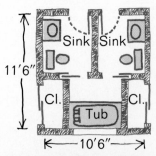

Three people *could use this bath at the same time; two closets fit compactly.*

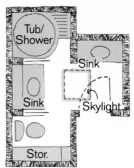

Plan: *Made private by pocket doors, three-room bath can serve four people.*

Open shelves *store towels; cabinet-top chute takes clothes right to the laundry room.*

Three-room bath *was arranged so vanities are in the outer compartment, tub and toilet in the other two. For privacy, you just pull the pocket doors shut. Counters, floor, and the tub/shower stall are surfaced with tile and trimmed with treated oak or teak.*

Three-room bath works well for four

When the alarm fails to ring and everybody is rushing to be on time for work and school, the three-room bath above is a welcome complex because four people can use it at once. Simple sliding pocket doors close off the outer compartment (where the washbasins are) from two side compartments. One of them contains a circular shower and spa; the other houses the toilet, storage shelves, and a laundry chute.

To keep clutter at a minimum, the bathroom was designed with plenty of storage space both below and behind the basins. Wide mirrors and white walls reflect light from an overhead skylight to keep the room bright and cheery all day long.

Architect: Douglas R. Zuberbuhler.

Bubble baths *are delicious in the deep circular tile tub, which is equipped with whirlpool jets. If you'd rather shower, you can do that, too; the tub doubles as a shower stall.*

THESE TUBS ARE SPECIAL

Mosaic pelicans, *the sun, the moon, and the tree of life dress a concrete tub that was poured with the house foundation. Colorful mosaics were set in 12-inch-wide sections and then pressed into mortar; bricks line the tub rim. Design: Martin Metal.*

Penny-round tile tub, *a variation on Japanese baths big enough for two, has a view of the trees through a striking circular window. The tub was built with sheets of the tiny tiles mortared and grouted over a metal pan. The pan had been coated with hot-asphalt-mopped roofing felt and chicken wire. Architects: Burger and Coplans.*

Dramatic soaking tub *was made of copper cut and soldered at a sheet-metal shop. Underneath the tub— it measures 5 feet across and 22 inches deep—are layers of sheet plastic, rigid insulation, and tar. Architect: J. Alexander Riley.*

Wood-framed tub, *tucked into an alcove when an upstairs bath was remodeled, is twice the size of a standard tub. The frame is redwood, treated with a polyurethane sealer and finish to increase its water resistance. Wide enough to allow insulation around the tub, the ledge also makes a handy bathroom bench. Architect: Robert Herman.*

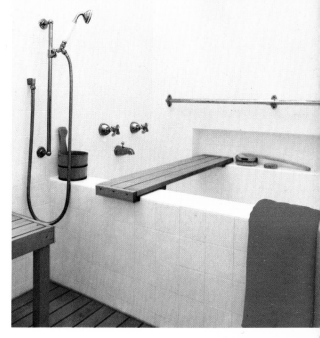

European-Japanese *bath lets you scrub down on the cedar bench before you soak in the starch-white tile tub. Architect: Robert B. Marquis.*

Smooth stones *surface a freeform tub that bends around the base of a 6-foot-high retaining wall. Stones were mortared over a steel-reinforced concrete shell. Redwood walls and ceiling add to the natural mood. Design: John Morrall, David F. Griffith.*

Handbuilt *of laminated 2 by 4s, this redwood tub was installed over a reinforced foundation and finished with five coats of spar varnish. Its floor is plywood, coated with fiberglass resin. Design: Chuck Jaeger.*

SEVEN IDEAS
FOR SHOWERS

Inside the triangular *tile shower and spa, bathers have a grand but private view outdoors when they open blinds along the window wall. Built into one end of the master bath, the spacious tub/shower has a clear shower curtain on a ceiling track. Architect: Michael Ellsner.*

Curving glass block shower *shows dramatic use of a building material that's making a comeback. Here, the clear, wavy blocks partition but don't obscure, so they let light into a compartment that might otherwise be dark. Installed in the same way as concrete blocks—with horizontal and vertical reinforcement—glass blocks are available in various sizes and patterns through some salvage yards, glass dealers, and building suppliers. Design: Tony Subbiondo.*

Stained glass *brightens a combination shower and bathing room that's linked to a "dry" bathroom with a sliding door. Walls are surfaced with treated tongue-and-groove cedar, the floor with 6-inch quarry tiles. Architect: Daniel M. Streissguth. Window design: Jean Frantz.*

Shower heads *spraying water fore and aft in tile shower and tub allow for quick and thorough soaking. Steps lead into tub; ledge at end holds plants. Architects: Clement Chen & Associates.*

Like a busy carwash *with water coming from every direction, copper-piped shower by the sauna has three heads, each with its own control valve. Designer: Al Garvey.*

Strong, sturdy, *and inexpensive panels of corrugated galvanized steel come indoors and into the bath. Shower panels were pop-riveted together, and silicon was caulked between the joints. A flat, custom-made panel covers the wall on which shower head and faucets are mounted. Architect: William P. Bruder.*

Camouflage the shower rod

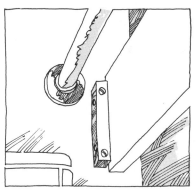

For a quick spruce-up of an old bathroom, try hiding the shower rod with a decorated length of 1 by 6 fir cut to fit the space. This one was cut from a piece of kiln-dried wood (it won't warp), carefully sealed, and then painted white. A simple house-and-tree design, first lightly sketched in pencil, was applied with acrylic paints. Then the board was mounted to the wall outside the shower curtain with 1 by 1s screwed both to the side of the board and to the wall. Designer: Melinda Barth.

WAYS TO STRETCH SPACE IN SMALL AND HALF-BATHS

Compact 4 by 4 bath maintains barrier-free space through use of teak grate over a drainage pan in the shower; clear shower curtain runs on a circular ceiling track. Tongue-and-groove cedar walls and ceiling were glued at the joints and finished with five coats of marine paint. Designer: John Weese.

Horizontal redwood walls and overhead mirrors create a feeling of greater space in a windowless 4 by 7-foot bath. Clear glass shower doors separate the shower from the rest of the room, yet preserve visual continuity of the uninterrupted quarry tile floor. Other streamlining features of this little bath include a sliding pocket door and a towel rack built between wall studs. Architect: Dartmond Cherk.

Three basic half-baths

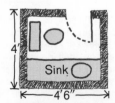

Positioning the two fixtures on different walls frees space for long counter.

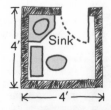

Corner lavatory saves about 6 inches of wall space in this square bathroom.

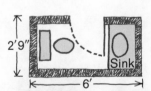

Simple rectangular bath might fit in a former closet or other narrow space.

Making space with light, white... and a dash of color

With the exception of strategic splashes of color on the walls and shower floor, white sets the tone for two little half-baths joined by swinging louvered doors. The baths, each measuring only 4 by 7 feet, share a skylight and ledge for plants that grow into both rooms. Walls and floor are painted stucco; in the alcove shower, handmade tiles are mortared into a freeform pattern.

Architect: Gene Henning.

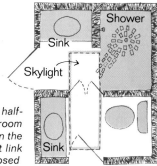

Plan: *Neighboring half-baths become powder room and shower room when the louvered doors that link them are closed*

White stucco walls *and skylight give the illusion of spaciousness to two half-baths inspired by the splendid white architecture of the Mediterranean. Here a little color—in the framed print and handmade tiles on the shower floor—goes a long way. Spotlights on dimmers and mirrors that swing out from the wall keep the rooms sophisticated but functional.*

Small bath with an upright tub

Switching from a standard tub to a short but deep soaking tub (it's only about 3 feet square and 3 feet deep) was one of the choices homeowners made when they turned a pantry-size room (only 7 feet square) into a functional guest bath. Made of fiberglass, the tub has a built-in seating ledge so you can stretch out in a sitting position.

For maximum space efficiency, owners pushed out an exterior wall so that a corner basin and shallow counter (with storage space below) could be added.

Architect: William B. Remick.

Short but deep *soaking tub saves space in a small guest bath. Here you can choose between a leisurely soak and a more perfunctory shower.*

Space-saving corner basin *and shallow counter (it's only a foot deep) make the bath seem a little less tight.*

51

SPECIAL EFFECTS WITH BATHROOM BASINS

Reglazed pedestal basin acquires a new, graceful quality, especially with its exposed plumbing. Mirror, accessories are in the same old-fashioned mood. Architect: William Kirsch.

Sleek hardwood basin and counter are one, created from lengths of 2 by 8-inch oak. The basin was sawed out of the oak boards before they were assembled and laminated to form the counter, then chiseled and sanded to shape. Fifteen fastidiously applied coats of glossy polyurethane seal the basin. The entire unit rests on reflective chrome legs. Architect: Richard Dorman.

Kitchen sink, big enough to make hair washing a snap, replaced a smaller fixture in a bathroom corner. Beautifully detailed woodworking enriches the basin area. Designers: John Morrall and David F. Griffith.

Blue and white chinoiserie basin matches the wallpaper; fittings have the look of pewter. Here, restricting the number of colors used in a bathroom to two produced a sophisticated look. Architect: Henry Blackard.

Hammered copper basin, the owner's second attempt at copper work, was shaped by heating sheet copper with an acetylene torch to make it malleable, hammering it, and then crimping the edges. Architect: J. Alexander Riley.

Stainless steel basin was manufactured as a bar sink, and its clean-lined control levers were intended for hospital use. Architect: Peter Behn.

Hand-thrown ceramic basin blends nicely with the oak counter in which it rests. Rounded wooden towel bar extends along front of counter. Designer: Eric Norstad.

SIX IDEAS FOR BATHROOM STORAGE

More storage *surrounds the toilet; shelf hinges up for access to tank. Built-in, metal-lined planter holds potted plants that thrive under the high-up skylight. Neat triangular shelves add convenience to tub/shower.*

Corner basin *saves space; long edge of counter visually enlarges room. Floor, counter, and tub are tiled; wood trim is mostly red oak with some maple. Wood rungs of towel ladder were recessed in the studs.*

Storage fits everywhere in small bath

Here the most pressing problem was the lack of ventilation and natural light. A room added on in a previous remodeling project had rendered useless the existing small window.

Minor structural modifications totally changed the bathroom. The useless window was covered over; an opening up through the attic allowed installation of a high, dramatic skylight that brings in light and creates a feeling of vertical space.

The owners did the painting themselves and contracted the rest of the work.

Architect: Michael D. Moyer.

Specially shaped drawers *fit into triangular cabinet. Scale-in-a-drawer pulls out from below.*

Tall cabinet *of drawers provides ample storage in a small corner. Designer: Carol Gordon.*

Deep wood drawers *look like office filing cabinets but store towels and bath paraphernalia. Here, drawers are handsomely framed into an angled tile wall at one end of the bathtub. Architect: Richard Dorman.*

Easy-to-build bathroom shelving

A shelving system that's assembled with dowel pegs may be just the boost your bathroom needs to put itself in order. What's nice about this system is its modular versatility: though it's designed with open shelving to fit over a toilet, you could build it with a cabinet and low shelves to fit against an extra wall, adjust its height to suit a nook, or make a double-width unit with shelves that share center uprights.

To make the shelving, you'll need a pencil, measuring tape, combination square, saw, electric drill, 1-inch spade or expansion bit, ¼-inch bit, large nail or center punch, hammer, screwdriver, and, if you have one, a drill press.

Using knot-free lumber, cut all pieces to size (before you buy the doweling, test-fit it into a 1-inch hole drilled in scrap lumber). Then, laying the 2 by 3s next to each other and butting them against something square, use your combination square to mark for 1-inch holes every 6 inches along their lengths, beginning 10½ inches from one end. Then set the square to exactly half the width of the 2 by 3 (about 1¼ inches) and mark the center of each hole placement line. Mark the center point with a nail or pointed tool. Next, mark and center-punch the 2 by 2 shelf supports (measure exactly 6¾ inches between hole centers) and both ends of the 1-inch dowels (allow exactly 1¼ inches between hole centers and dowel ends).

The trickiest part is drilling the holes—you must take care to drill them neat and straight so the dowels fit properly. (For drilling tips and instructions, see the *Sunset* book *How to Make Bookshelves & Cabinets.*)

After all the holes are drilled, sand the ends of the dowels and all sides of the other shelving members and apply a polyurethane sealer or other water-resistant finish. Screw the appliance levelers to T-nuts attached to the upright members, then assemble the unit and set it up, checking for level and plumb. Designer: Donald W. Vandervort.

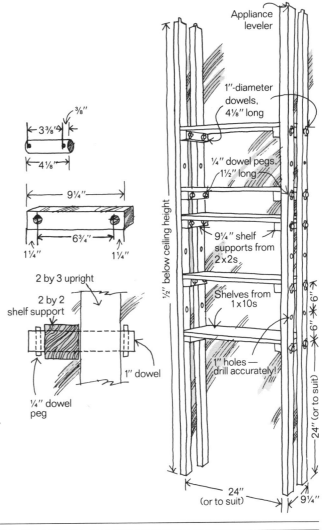

Accessorizing the bath
with towel bars and paper holders

Cutout for towels *eliminates need for extra towel bar. Architect: Michael J. Soldano.*

Over-and-under towel racks, *one for adults and one for kids, are easily assembled with horizontal 2 by 2s and 4½-inch-long 2 by 3s mounted to each other and to the wall with 6-inch-long lag bolts.*

Box library in the bathroom

Handy little library built into the bathroom wall was made with Douglas fir and plastic-laminate-covered plywood (painted plywood would work just as well). Box sides have butt joints; holes drilled halfway through the sides (before assembly) hold the dowel. The completed unit was then slipped into a hole cut in the wall and side-nailed to a wall stud. Added molding is mitered at the corners. Designer: John Schmid.

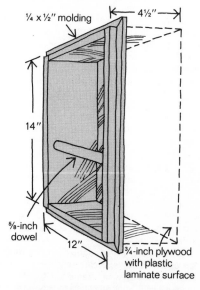

¼ x ½" molding

4½"

14"

⅝-inch dowel

12"

¾-inch plywood with plastic laminate surface

Simple box *built into the wall can serve as a handy bathroom library.*

You can adjust *the size to suit your space requirements. Nail and glue together; finish with polyurethane or paint.*

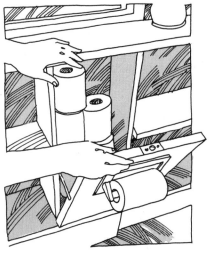

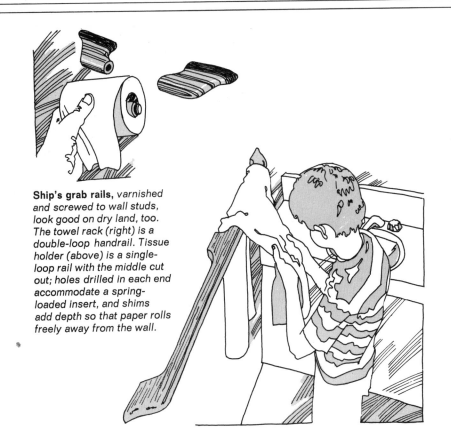

Ship's grab rails, *varnished and screwed to wall studs, look good on dry land, too. The towel rack (right) is a double-loop handrail. Tissue holder (above) is a single-loop rail with the middle cut out; holes drilled in each end accommodate a spring-loaded insert, and shims add depth so that paper rolls freely away from the wall.*

Concealed *behind tissue holder, compartment stores eight more rolls. Architects: Akiyama, Kekoolani.*

Easy-to-make hook, towel bar, paper holder

All three of the accessories shown took only a few hours to make and install, and the materials cost under $5. Cut from ¾-inch oak board and beveled along the edges with a power saw or sander, these holders were finished with several coats of clear polyurethane sealer and attached to the walls with glue and dowels.

For each device, bevel all edges except the side that fits against the wall. To attach, drill holes in each bracket and in the wall large enough to accept short lengths of ¼-inch doweling (two pieces of dowel for each bracket). Glue and set as in sketch. Designer: Gordon Hammond.

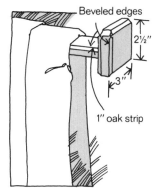

To assemble towel bar, *place the end of the rod on the bracket, trace its outline with a pencil, and chisel out about ¼ inch. Then attach one bracket to the wall and hold the towel bar in place in its socket while you position the other.*

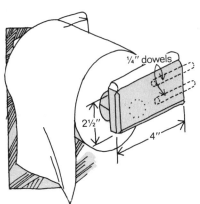

Paper-holder brackets *have slightly oversize holes centered 1 inch from the inside edge to hold a spring-loaded insert available at hardware stores.*

Hook *is easily made from scrap lumber. Attach it to the wall with blind dowels, as the sketch at left shows.*

BATHROOM LIGHTING AND MIRRORS

Overhead mirror *reflects light into the basin area, eliminating shadows—and it seems to stretch the ceiling line. Designer: Priscilla Fontana.*

Create myriad reflections *and an apparently endless stream of lights by placing mirrors on three sides of vanity. Incandescent theatrical light bulbs provide accurate, shadowless illumination. Designer: Bill Nilsen.*

Side lighting *comes from light boxes recessed in the walls and screened with doors made of wood slats and translucent plastic.*

Fluorescent tubes *mounted in boxes above and at sides of a mirror provide the basin area with even, energy-efficient illumination. Architects: Johnson, Reese, Luersen, and Lowrey.*

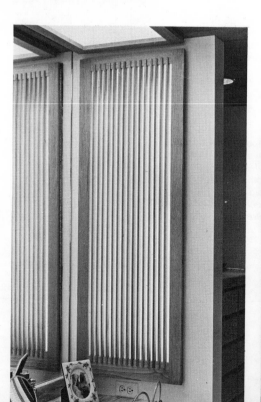

58

Black trim *accents hexagonal mirror, edge of skylight, cabinet, and a sliding door that's hung on tracks, barn-door style.*

Standard greenhouse glass sections, *installed in a row high above the bathroom counter, let in plenty of light all day long. Whenever the light becomes too strong, matchstick shades can be drawn over the glass panels. Vents open for fresh air. Architect: Peter Behn.*

BATHING IN
THE WARMTH
OF WOOD

Even the tub is wood *in this cedar-paneled bathroom that stars a recycled stained-glass window. Insulated with fiberglass batting, the tub was made waterproof with fiberglass cloth and several coats of resin (see page 7). Walls are protected with plastic oil sealer that can be reapplied following periodic scrubdowns with liquid dish soap and a stiff brush. Designer: Rick Morrall.*

Handsome pine cabinetry *disguises a generous laundry bin that rolls out from under the basin. Continuous drawer pulls produce the trim, uncluttered look. (See page 33 for full bathroom view.) Architect: James K. Bell.*

Ceiling-high storage unit, *with three sets of doors, has adjustable, lipped shelves inside the doors for all the miscellany that collects in a medicine cabinet. Highest shelves are well out of children's reach. Architect: James K. Bell.*

Rough Douglas fir *paneling installed horizontally makes the vanity appear wider. Flush with one wall are a hinged medicine cabinet and adjacent linen closet; below the oak counter are baskets for towels and laundry. Skylight brings in natural light, enhancing the warm wood tones. Architect: Herbert D. Kosovitz.*

Recycled redwood *boards, salvaged from feed troughs and patched with pieces of tin, give a rustic feeling to a bath remodeled around original fixtures. Over the sink— an old soy tub made of naturally water-resistant teak—is a delightful plumbing sculpture of narrow copper pipes and faucets arranged one above the other. Designer: Al Garvey.*

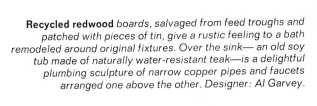

DECORATING FOR A CUSTOM LOOK

Full-length curtains *and harmonizing wallpaper convert an ordinary bathroom into one of distinctive sophistication. Even the dullest bathroom can take on a bright new look with wallpaper and complementary fabric... and often at reasonable cost. Designer: Jean Chappell.*

Wonderfully dappled wildflowers *are permanently fixed in a countertop mural. The tiles and basins are handmade porcelain. Designer: Cindy Haug.*

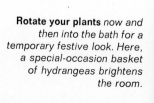

Rotate your plants *now and then into the bath for a temporary festive look. Here, a special-occasion basket of hydrangeas brightens the room.*

Permanently luxuriant ferns, *handpainted on cream-colored tile, "grow" on the walls around a standard tub. Designer: Barbara Vantrease Beall Studio.*

Raindrops are falling *down a delightful shower curtain made from a full-size sheet. The drops were applied with a fusible bonding, then machine-stitched to the sheet and, temporarily, to pieces of paper that prevent puckering. Curtain and buttonholes were matched to a plastic shower liner. Designer: Phyllis Dunston. Architect: William R. Boehm, Jr.*

Learning the language of bathroom color

When you enter a bathroom or when you glance at a photograph of one, color is the first thing you see. It speaks louder than form; it can create patterns and shapes independent of the basic structure of the room, change its apparent size and shape, join places that are separate, or divide a single surface. Small bathrooms can be made to appear spacious with a sweep of light, harmonizing colors. Oversize bathrooms decorated in dark tones can seem cozy, even intimate.

Let your own likes dictate the colors you choose for your bath. If you lean toward soft, muted colors, consider the natural tones found in New England architecture. If you like warm, bright colors, don't be afraid to experiment with salmon pink or a snappy yellow.

Whichever direction you go with color in your bath, a color wheel (found in art supply stores) can be most helpful. Colors that appear opposite each other on the wheel are *complementary.* In a complementary scheme, usually one color is used at full intensity. But look at the bathroom on page 44: the complementary colors blue and orange are used in quantities small enough that both can be used at full intensity. *Analogous* colors, on the other hand, are located next to each other on the color wheel. The yellows and oranges seen in the bathroom on page 68 represent an analogous color scheme.

Three colors equidistant from each other on the wheel—like primary red, yellow, and blue seen in the bathroom at the top of page 75—are called a *triad.* A *monochromatic* color scheme uses only one color—perhaps like the two shades of purple you see in the tile and carpeting on page 52—in several different tints or shades.

To avoid mistakes when you choose colors, view all the shades you're considering under the same type of light you'll have in the bathroom—colors appear to change under different lighting conditions—and view them with all coordinating materials, including wood, metals, and porcelain. Since we have no true color memory, it's important to have all samples together to make accurate judgments.

Because floors and countertops aren't changed very often, they should be selected carefully to harmonize with the color of the fixtures. The same is true of walls if they're to be surfaced with such permanent materials as ceramic tile. You can select colors more freely for painted walls, which generally need repainting every 4 or 5 years.

You might find your greatest freedom in using color when you decorate walls and choose accessories; with neutral fixtures and flooring, you can change towels and wall color whenever the mood strikes—tweedy beige to Chinese red.

GROW A GARDEN IN THE BATH

Little low window on a Hawaiian tree fern puts a living painting on the wall of a master bathroom. The fern reaches up to a trellis that lets in partial sun; richly detailed redwood fencing lends privacy. Architects: Johnson, Reese, Luersen & Lowrey. Landscape Designer: Jack Kawamoto.

Spacious shower room opens at one end to the dressing area and at the other to a skylighted planter. In the planter bed grow a row of hardy Dieffenbachia amoena (dumb cane) and a towering Ficus elastica (rubber plant). Both species grow well where they can get ample indirect light.

Beside a sunken tub, a jungle of hanging and floor plants thrives in the bathroom's moisture and humidity. Container gardens such as this let you rotate plants and add fresh splashes of color to the bathroom as flowering species come into bloom. The plants here are protected from direct sun by a high, white-painted masonry wall. Architect: Richard Caviness.

Step out of the tub *into a garden that's accessible through louvered bifold doors. Enclosed by a wood fence with overhead screening, the garden brings the outdoors right into the room. Architects: Belt Collins & Assoc. Ltd.*

Skylight garden *has two vigorous Nephrolepis exaltata 'Bostoniensis' (Boston ferns) suspended from beams above the bathroom basin. Plants in an interior window box receive still more light from a side window. Here's a good example of how just a few judiciously placed plants can add a splash of style. Architects: Moyer Associates.*

These plants thrive in the bathroom

A sunny, humid bathroom can be the best environment in the house for nurturing plants. But each bathroom will offer slightly different growing conditions. Most bathrooms are a bit warmer than the rest of the house and have a comparatively lower light level and a higher, but varying, humidity level.

The following plants are suited to the conditions in an average bathroom. For detailed information on how to grow them refer to the *Sunset* gardening books.

Aglaonema (includes Chinese evergreen)

Anthurium

Ardisia crenata (coral berry)

Aspidistra elatior (cast-iron plant)

Asplenium (includes mother fern, bird's nest fern)

Begonia (foliage varieties)

Calathea

Callisia elegans (striped inch plant)

Chamaedorea

Cissus (includes grape ivy, dwarf kangaroo ivy)

Coffea arabica (coffee tree)

Colocasia esculenta (taro, elephant's ear)

Columnea

Cryptanthus zonatus

Ctenanthe

Cyrtomium falcatum (holly fern)

Dieffenbachia (dumb cane, mother-in-law plant)

Guzmania lingulata

Hedyscepe canterburyana

Howea (kentia palm)

Hypoestes sanguinolenta

Maranta leuconeura (prayer plant, rabbit tracks)

Monstera deliciosa (split-leaf philodendron)

Nertera granadensis (bead plant)

Nidularium innocentii

Pellaea (cliff brake, button fern)

Peperomia

Philodendron

Phoenix roebelenii (pigmy date palm)

Plectranthus (Swedish ivy)

Polypodium aureum (hare's foot fern)

Polystichum

Rhaphidophora aurea (devil's ivy, silver pothos)

Rhapis (lady palm)

Rhipsalidopsis gaertneri (Easter cactus)

Rhipsalis paradoxa (rice cactus)

Rhoeo spathacea (Moses-in-the-cradle)

Ruellia makoyana (trailing velvet plant)

Sansevieria (bowstring hemp, snake plant)

Saxifraga stolonifera (strawberry geranium)

Selaginella (moss fern, spike moss)

Sparmannia africana (African linden)

Spathiphyllum

Syngonium podophyllum (arrowhead plant)

Tradescantia fluminensis (wandering Jew)

MORE THAN A BATH...ENJOY A RIBBSTOL, SAUNA, OR SOAKING TUB

Exercise unit is a Swedish ribbstol

It works for sit-ups, leg lifts, elevated push-ups, ballet *barre* exercises, and for children who just like to scramble up and down. This sturdy piece of Swedish exercise equipment, called a *ribbstol* (pronounced rib-stool), shares bathroom space and offers serious exercisers a spot to work out. It was built of fir 2 by 6s and fourteen 3-foot lengths of pine dowels, then bolted securely to the wall studs.

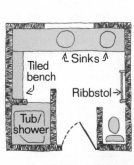

Plan: *Bathroom addition, 11 feet square, has room for a Swedish ribbstol. Tiled bench provides a dressing area outside the combination tub/shower.*

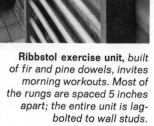

Ribbstol exercise unit, *built of fir and pine dowels, invites morning workouts. Most of the rungs are spaced 5 inches apart; the entire unit is lag-bolted to wall studs.*

You can climb around *the Swedish ribbstol and still not take up too much space in this 11-foot-square bathroom. Adjacent to a twin-basin vanity, the ribbstol needs about the same wall space as a towel bar.*

Special room for just a good, hot bath

Wanting a choice between the hot "dry" bath of the Finnish sauna and the hot "wet" bath of the Japanese soaking tub, owners had both built into a new bathroom during a major remodeling project. Sandwiched between tub and sauna is a handsome oval shower, where bathers first soap and rinse. Adjacent to the bath, through sliding shoji screens, is a resting room floored with Japanese tatami mats.

Architect: Douglas R. Zuberbuhler.

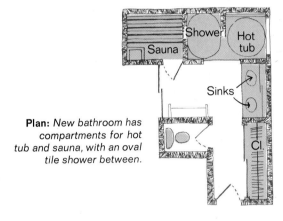

Plan: *New bathroom has compartments for hot tub and sauna, with an oval tile shower between.*

Spacious new master bathroom *invites you for a hot dry bath in the Finnish sauna or a hot wet bath in the redwood hot tub. Bench outside the sauna provides a place to rest between visits to the baths.*

Oval tile shower *and redwood tub share a semi-enclosed compartment. Low faucets and Japanese bathing tools in the shower remind you to scrub down before you enter the hot tub.*

Fold back the wooden lid *and slide into the steamy hot water. The hot tub, equipped with hydrojets, was installed at floor level over a galvanized metal pan with drainage to household waste lines.*

HOT TUBS, SPAS, AND SAUNAS

Plan: *Spare bedroom was transformed into a garden bath, with oversize tub and skylighted reading alcove. The new bath includes an open shower and storage wall and has access to the deck outdoors.*

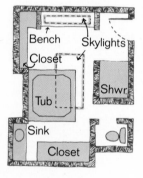

Immense, spa-like tub *sits right in the middle of a luxurious master bath that was converted from a seldom-used bedroom. Made of fiberglass and measuring 5 by 7 feet, the tub has a wallboard box frame and insulation to keep the water warm. Designers: Paul H. and Jane W. Juliet.*

Sunken tile spa *is the focal point of an expanded master bath that was surfaced with off-white tile and dark grout. The spa has shower fittings at one end, a window wall at the other. Designers: Don Brandeu and Clara G. Kurgan.*

Slabs of recycled slate *make a bold and handsome surface for the floor and sunken spa in this dramatic brick-walled bath. Smooth and durable, the slate was mortared over a concrete foundation. Architect: Charles W. Delk.*

Hand-built *of barn wood and mortared stone, this large sauna incorporates several square-paned windows. Benches at two levels let you choose between moderate and high heat. Woodworking by Frank Bitz; stonework by Allan Elder.*

High, narrow window *lets light into a sauna surfaced with light-colored fir. Wood railing shields a wood-burning heater. Designer: Forrest Shute.*

Outdoor bathhouse *has both hot tub and sauna, with shower between. The half-sunken tub is 6 feet in diameter and 4 feet deep; from it, bathers can view a private garden. Designers: Dolphin Woodworks and Maroto Imai.*

Plan: *Sauna complex includes a shower for cooling down and benches for resting. Towels are stored below the benches outside the sauna; wood for the heater has its own storage compartment.*

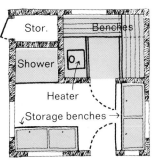

Stor.

Benches

Shower

Heater

Storage benches

THE JAPANESE BATH

Freestanding teak furo *sits in a tiled shower room fitted with drain. Inside the tub is a contoured seat; exterior extension becomes a step. Oversize pipes from the water heater increase water pressure to fill tub quickly. Designer: Arthur Hanna.*

Japanese bath merges, *as tradition dictates, with the natural world—here, an intimate garden. Within the cedar-paneled room are the furo (it too is cedar, measuring 4 feet square and 22 inches deep) and a shower. Japanese bathing tools, the oke (wooden bucket) and koshikake (wooden stool) are important accessories, for Japanese tradition also requires that bathers soap and rinse before slipping into the clean, hot water. Architect: Alfred Klyce.*

Beautifully finished teak *frames an occidental approach to the furo—a soaking tub surfaced with tile. Here, as in the wood tubs above, you can absorb the quiet, meditative atmosphere that characterizes the Japanese bath. Architect: Sohn & Nakahira.*

Serene indoor garden *lengthens a narrow bathing room and offers a pleasant view from the sunken furo. Architects: John Russell Rummell & Associates.*

Round fiberglass *soaking tub is tucked between shower stall and tiled dressing bench. Designer: Prudence Ducich.*

Circular furo, *with an oak bench and access ladder, is an adaptation of the free-standing tub. Incorporating whirlpool jets into the unit would make it a spa. Architect: Tracy Price.*

Inside the energy-efficient bath

Energy-saving tips for the bathroom

Old habits notwithstanding, increased demands on our energy supply, along with the rising costs of natural gas and electricity, are causing all of us to reevaluate the way we use our resources. Learning to modify our houses according to the climate and realizing how to use water, gas, and electricity wisely have become our tools for curbing energy consumption—and for cutting those climbing utility bills.

In the bathroom there are virtually dozens of ways to shorten your own rein on energy use. Some involve nothing more than learning new habits: taking a shower rather than a tub bath, for instance, can save you 2,000 gallons of hot water a year. Others require a few dollars and a Saturday afternoon's work to put an end to leaky faucets, install a water-flow restrictor in the shower head, caulk around the bathtub, and insulate the water heater.

If you're building or remodeling, consider including in your project some of the energy-efficient features illustrated below: electricity-saving skylights and fluorescent lighting, a water-saving toilet, and perhaps a solar-assisted heating system (it can provide more than 50 percent of your hot-water needs).

1. Insulate floors, walls, and ceiling to R-value specification for your area.
2. Install separate switches for lights, ventilation fan. Or put the fan on a timer.
3. Use warm-tone fluorescent lighting.
4. Install small-capacity point-of-use water heaters for basins in little-used bathrooms.
5. Install double or triple-glazed skylights to eliminate the need for electrical lights during the day.
6. Insulate hot-water pipes (see opposite).
7. Wrap an insulating blanket around your water heater; keep the thermostat no higher than 120°.
8. Link your water heater to solar collectors; they can provide more than 50 percent of your hot-water needs.
9. Install a low-flow shower head or water restrictor.
10. Caulk and weatherstrip around windows; caulk around bathtub rim.
11. Use double or triple-glazed windows.
12. Insulate around the tub.
13. Install a water-saving (or composting, if codes permit) toilet.
14. Cover floor with nonskid mats or carpeting.

Antique wood stove *supplements a conventional heating system to provide economical —and cozy—bathside warmth. Tile flooring satisfies the code requirement for noncombustible materials beneath the stove.*

Daylight floods *a new bathroom through angled louvered window and reduces the daytime demand on electricity. Louvers allow for natural ventilation. Architect: Stan Stratton.*

How to insulate hot-water pipes

While you wait for the water to turn hot in the tap, valuable water swirls down the drain—water that could have been warm if it were running through insulated pipes. You can save water—and the heat that's lost through exposed pipes—if you insulate hot-water pipes running through an unheated attic, basement, garage, or crawl space.

Use hot-water-pipe insulation available at most hardware stores and from plumbing and heating suppliers. Choose either sleeves of foam insulation that you cut to size and slip over pipes, or narrow rolls of fiberglass batting that you wrap loosely around the pipes and then cover with protective tape. When installing fiberglass insulation, be sure to wear a long-sleeved shirt, gloves, goggles and a face mask. Before installing either type, carefully read manufacturer's instructions.

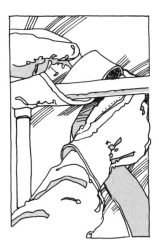

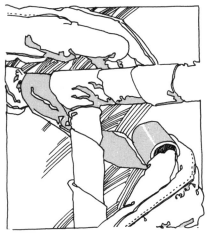

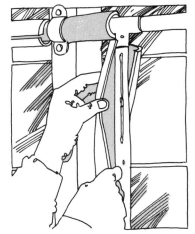

Fiberglass insulation *is loosely wrapped around pipes.*

Protective tape *covers fiberglass insulation.*

Foam insulation *is simply slipped over pipes.*

BRIGHT AND CHEERY CHILDREN'S BATHS

Pull-out steps *are simply plywood drawers used bottom-side-up to help children reach basins. Between basins, tilt-out clothes hamper has a dowel handle that doubles as a child-height towel bar.*

Just the right height *for a 3-year-old, mirror encourages hair combing, making faces. Adhesive pads hold mirror to wall.*

Colorful graphic *was painted once, shows up twice in a little boy's bathroom. Supergraphics like this one are especially effective in small bathrooms because they can give the room a feeling of greater height or width.*

Tips for making your bathroom safe

The fact that almost 200,000 children and adults are injured or disabled in bathroom-related accidents every year should be enough of a stimulus to head us toward the bathroom to weed out a carelessly kept medicine cabinet, put down slip-resistant mats in a potentially slippery bathtub, or put safety caps on unused electrical outlets. Though unfortunately it's impossible to create a perfectly safe bathroom, you can take steps to make yours safer. Here are some suggestions:

• Store all medicines well out of the sight and reach of children; a locked cabinet is best.

• Whenever possible, buy medicines and toxic household cleaners in childproof containers.

• Use safety latches on any drawers and cabinet doors that you'd like to keep "off limits" to young children.

• Take an inventory of your medicine cabinet once or twice a year; discard prescription medications no longer being used, plus any containers with unreadable labels.

• Post the telephone numbers of the nearest poison control center and rescue squad.

• Keep a first-aid chart taped to the door in the medicine cabinet, with a first-aid kit nearby.

• Never leave a small child alone in the bathtub; drownings can and do occur in less than the minute you might take to answer the telephone. If you need to leave the bathroom, wrap a towel around the youngster and take him or her with you.

• If your tub or shower doesn't have a slip-resistant finish, put down nonslip treads or a suction mat that can be removed to dry after each use.

• Install safety covers over any unused electrical outlets.

• Store appliances such as blow dryers and electric shavers out of children's reach and *never* permit electrically operated toys in the bathroom.

• On bathroom doors, install locks that can be opened from the outside in an emergency.

• Lower your water-heater thermostat to 115° or below. This will prevent painful scalds that can result from sudden bursts of hot water when cold water is diverted to another tap, as well as serious burns should your toddler decide to fill the tub herself. (You'll also save on your utility bill.)

• Be sure that tub and shower enclosures are made of shatter-resistant glass or plastic.

• In both showers and tubs, especially those used by older family members, put up grab bars that can support 250 pounds.

• Use nonskid bath mats, especially over tile floors.

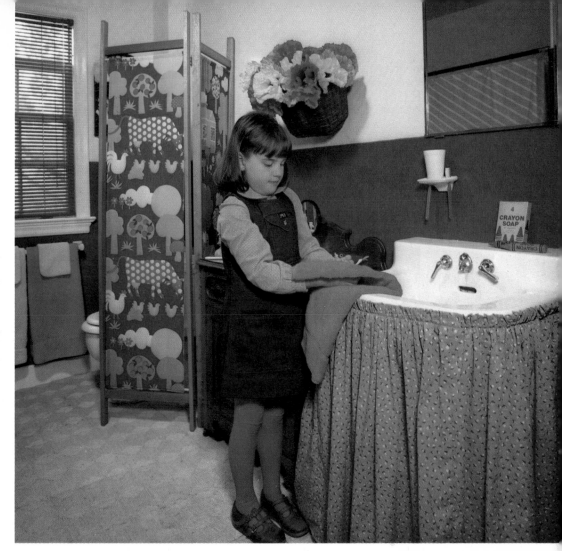

A little fabric and some bright blue paint give a cheery new look to an older bath. The fabric screen of barnyard animals partitions off the toilet, and a field of miniature flowers skirts the basin and hides the laundry basket. Shower curtain (see mirror reflection) is diagonally striped cotton over a plastic liner. Designer: Mary Martin.

Slick, banana-yellow walls and polka-dotted flooring brighten a bath for children. White counters and fixtures let you change the color scheme easily; later on, adding wallpaper and carpet could give you an elegant guest bath. Designers: Falls, Grant, Lucas, Inc.

INDOOR/OUTDOOR BATHS

Cantilevered bay window *gives a basic white bathtub a brand new look, while bather enjoys a sensational view into the trees. Tiled ledge makes room for an indoor garden as well. Designer: John Matthias.*

Outdoor tub *is really right in the garden where its owner can relax in a warm bath, rain or shine. Found in a wrecking yard for just $50, the old tub was painted on the outside with bright green epoxy paint, then hooked up to kitchen plumbing a few feet away. White lattice fencing ensures privacy.*

Soak in the sunken tub *and admire the colorful atrium garden. Fenced in, the garden gives the bath privacy. The wide window makes the bathroom seem larger. Designer: Sherri Waldman.*

Plan: *Window walls along two sides of a bathroom open it up to a wooded setting. Toilet compartment also is windowed to avoid a feeling of claustrophobia.*

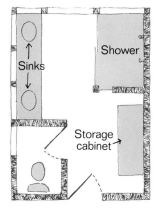

Ceiling-high windows *let you look outdoors, watch birds or squirrels from almost any spot in the bath. In window frames above the basins hang small wicker-framed mirrors. The vanity is oak.*

Window walls for a redwood setting

To open up their new home to surrounding redwood trees, owners had many of the rooms—including the master bath—designed with walls of ceiling-high windows. Framed with redwood, the bathroom windows offer grand views in two directions and let in a flood of natural light throughout the day. Ceiling fixtures and valance above the basins provide illumination after dark.
Architect: James K. Bell.

Glass-walled shower, *with two shower heads, repeats the theme of openness— bathers are treated to abundant light and splendid views.*

THREE STRIKING CONTEMPORARIES

It's almost futuristic, *this master bath with a tub/shower room you enter through a windowlike opening. Light comes into the bathing room through an overhead skylight; heat lamps warm the adjoining drying compartment. Skylighted lavatory room has a towel-rack ladder that leads to overhead storage. Architect: Wendell Lovett.*

Smashing, cherry-colored *tiles dramatize a sunken tub and adjacent shower in a skylighted master bath. Bathers have a view of an adjacent greenhouse garden; overhead, starch-white shades can be drawn to control light. Architect: Bert W. Tarayao.*

Elliptical tomato-red vanity *makes a startling focal point in a split-level bathroom. From either basin in the freestanding unit, you can peer into a circular mirror suspended from the ceiling. Overhead spotlights are aimed directly downward. Architect: Wendell Lovett.*

A glossary of useful terms

Aerator. Small device that mixes air with water as water flows out of the spout; minimizes splashes.

Basin. A fixture that makes water available for washing hands and face. Also called "lavatory" or "sink."

Bath, receptor. A small, low tub, occupying about the same floor area as a large shower, used primarily as a shower base or a child's bath.

Bath, recessed. A tub designed to be enclosed by walls on three sides.

Bidet. A small tub for washing the perineal area.

Brass. Generic term for fittings, regardless of the material of which they're made.

Brass, solid. Fittings in which all metal parts are brass. Surface may be chrome-plated in either a brushed or polished finish.

Cast iron, enameled. Fixture material; iron is cast in one piece and then enameled while red-hot so enamel fuses to the cast iron.

China, vitreous. Compounded ceramic material fired at high temperature; resistant to corrosion and discoloration; used for fixtures.

Code, plumbing. Rules established by a sanitation authority to regulate materials and methods of installing plumbing.

Diverter valve. Valve that changes water flow from one outlet to another, such as from a bath spout to the shower head.

Drain. A pipe carrying waste water in a house drainage system.

Enamel. Glasslike finish for vitreous china, cast-iron, and formed steel fixtures.

Fiberglass. A material used for fixtures; a lamination of liquid polyester resins interspersed with thin glass fibers.

Fittings. Mechanical devices for the control of water entering or leaving the fixture—for instance, faucets, spouts, drain controls, diverter valves for tubs and basins.

Fitting, centerset. A single-unit basin fitting (containing handles and spout) that is surface mounted on top ledge of a basin or on a counter.

Fixtures, plumbing. Devices such as tubs, toilets, and basins that receive water or make it available, or receive liquid or waterborne waste and discharge the wastes into a drainage system.

Float valve. A device that automatically regulates the amount of water in a toilet flush tank. Also referred to as a "ball cock."

Flush valve. A device for flushing toilets or similar fixtures.

Half-bathroom. Bathroom equipped with basin and toilet only; without tub or shower.

Ledge back. A flat elevation at the back of a basin, less than 2 inches above the rim and usually extending the full length of the fixture. Brass fittings are customarily mounted on the ledge.

Overflow. Outlet for escape of water in a tub or basin to prevent flooding of bathroom if water is left on.

Pipe, fixture supply. Pipe that brings water from behind the wall to a plumbing fixture. Also called "supply."

Pipe, soil. A pipe that carries the discharge from toilets and often from the other fixtures, too. Often called "soil stack."

Pipe, vent. A pipe installed to provide a flow of air to or from a drainage system or to provide air circulation within such a system; protects trap seals from siphonage and back pressure.

Pipe, waste. A line that carries discharge from any fixture except toilets and conveys it to the building drain or waste stack.

Pressure regulator. Installed between house plumbing and main water supply to regulate water pressure.

Rim, antisplash. Lip on inside front of basin; minimizes water splashing out of bowl.

Roughing in. Installation of concealed piping (in walls and floor) to which supply lines and drain from a plumbing fixture are attached.

Self-rimming. Basin designed for counter installation without metal mounting frame.

Shelf back. A flat elevation at the back of a basin, higher than 2 inches above the rim and extending the full fixture length.

Siphon jet. Most expensive and efficient type of toilet.

Spout, diverter. Tub filler spout (part of a bath and shower fitting) in which a knob is lifted to divert water from the spout to the shower head.

Stack. Main vertical pipe of a system of soil, waste, or vent piping.

Steel, enameled formed. A material for fixtures; sheets of steel are formed and finished with baked-on porcelain enamel.

Supply. Pipe that brings water from behind the wall to a plumbing fixture.

Trap. A bent pipe section or other device that holds a water deposit and forms a seal against the passage of sewer gasses.

Vacuum breaker. A device to prevent waste water backflow into a water-supply line.

Valve seat, integral. A pipe venting a trap or waste pipe beneath or behind a fixture served by it, and connected to the main vent at a point above the fixture.

Vent stack. A vertical pipe, sometimes called the "main vent," that provides circulation of air to and from any part of the drainage system.

Waste. Fitting through which water from bath or basin flows into waste pipe.

Waste, chain and stopper. Water is retained in basin or tub by means of a rubber stopper. Stopper chain is usually attached to the spout.

Waste, pop-up. A mechanically operated metal stopper that retains water in basin or tub.

Waste, trip lever. Tub stopper that prevents the flow of water out of the pipe below the tub by means of a plunger.

Water closet. Toilet. Abbreviated "W. C."

Wet venting. Plumbing system in which one vertical pipe is used for both venting and draining waste water.

Wet wall. Wall containing supply lines and soil and waste pipes.

Index

Photographers

Edward Bigelow: 34 bottom, 35, 36 bottom right, 37, 38 bottom left & right, 39, 46 top left, 47 top & bottom left, 53 top left, center left, & bottom, 54, 59 left, 61, 69, 71 right, 76 left. **Jeremiah O. Bragstad:** 36 top right. **Glenn Christiansen:** 34 top left, 52 left, 70 top left. **David Cornwell:** 71 top. **Walt Dibblee:** 18. **Richard Fish:** 14 bottom left, 47 bottom right, 48 top right, 55 left, 63 right, 71 bottom, 78 left. **Jerry Fredrick:** 27, 65 right. **Art Hupy:** 14 bottom right. **Leonard Koren:** 14 top. **Edmund Y. Lee:** 74 left. **Fred Lyon:** 59 right. **Jack McDowell:** 33, 40, 41, 42, 43, 44, 48 left, 51, 60 bottom, 62 left, 63 left, 67, 68 top & bottom right, 70 top right & bottom, 75, 77. **Steve W. Marley:** 62 top, 76 bottom. **Philip Molten:** 46 top right, 53 center right. **Stewart Morton:** 36 bottom left. **Don Normark:** 48 bottom, 49 right, 64 top left, 74 right. **Norman A. Plate:** 8 right, 17, 34 top right, 52 right, 55 right, 58 bottom, 60 top, 64 top right & bottom, 76 top right. **Bill Ross:** 66. **Hal Ross:** 8 left. **Rob Super:** 45, 78 top right & bottom. **Darrow M. Watt:** 13, 15, 31, 36 top left, 38 top, 46 bottom, 47 top right, 49 top left & bottom, 50, 58 top left & right, 68 left, 74 center. **Wenkam/Salbosa:** 65 left. **Michael Wright:** 38 center. **Tom Wyatt:** 62 bottom. **Craig Zwicky:** 7.